Famous Houses
of the
West Country

Famous Houses of the West Country

Charles Greenwood

Kingsmead Press

First published in 1977 by
Kingsmead Press,
Rosewell House
Kingsmead Square
Bath

© Charles Greenwood, 1977

SBN 901571 87 3

Text set in 12 pt Photon Times, printed by photolithography, and
bound in Great Britain at The Pitman Press, Bath

Contents

Introduction

Only by setting certain limits is it possible to deal with so vast a subject as the Historic Houses of Avon, Somerset, Wiltshire and Gloucestershire within a single volume. Even within the limits I set myself the treatment cannot be anything like comprehensive, for with scores of charming mansions to select from; there are many of them scattered all over the West Country, the only practical course was to accept those which gave access to the public.

In writing this book I make no pretence at scholarship, but to convey simply how these historic houses and the families that lived in them have helped to create the pageant that has become England's history. It has been said so many times before that history is more about people than about events. I hope the stories I relate in the book will justify it.

Enormous difficulties have been faced by the owners of these beautiful houses in trying to preserve their inheritance, and it is their great sense of responsibility that enables them to carry on. The National Trust has taken on the role as custodian of many of these houses, but even with the resources of the Trust it is difficult to keep up with the ever recurring problem of soaring costs.

I must thank my good friend and fellow photographer Ralph Warfield of the Stothert and Pitt Camera Club, who has supplied so many of the photographs used in the text, and thanks are due to the Bath and West Evening Chronicle in allowing me to use their photograph of Wade's House in Abbey Churchyard, and photograph of Ralph Allen's Town House supplied by Brian Davis, Dept of Architecture & Planning, Bath City Council. Acknowledgements are due to the National Trust for the help I found in referring to the "National Trust Guide", and to Walter Ison's "The Georgian Buildings of Bath", the most comprehensive book on Bath's architecture.

Charles Greenwood

If in doubt about the opening times of any of the houses mentioned the Bath Information Bureau would be only too pleased to assist.

Barrington Court
Near Ilminster, Somerset

Situated among the hill woodlands of the mid-Somerset countryside and only a short distance north-east from Ilminster lies the Tudor mansion of Barrington Court, the one time home of Henry, Lord Daubeny, whose family had lived in this corner of Somerset since the Conquest. The d'Aubigne's settled here in the 12th century and acquired the manors of Barrington and South Petherton, and when Richard, Earl of Cornwall started scouring the West Country for men-at-arms to follow him on the Crusades to the Holy Land, it was Philip d'Aubigne who joined him and died later fighting in the Holy Land.

The manors passed eventually to Sir Ralph Daubeny, who with his elder son Sir Philip fought alongside Edward I in his attempt to annex Wales. The Daubenys as king's men were not wanting when it came to espousing the loyal cause, one named Sir Ralph fought with Edward III at Crecy, whilst Sir Giles who succeeded to the estates in 1401 fought for Henry V in France. His son William lived at South Petherton and built a mansion there which now no longer exists, he had a son, another Giles, who played an important role in the defeat of Richard III and the establishment of Henry of Richmond – later Henry VII – on the throne. Unfortunately at first this struggle turned sour, Daubeny lost the Barrington estates to the crown in 1483, and Henry having reached Poole found that Richard's supporters were too strong, and so he retired to France temporarily, taking Daubeny with him.

Later under Henry VII Giles Daubeny was created a peer and became Lord Chamberlain, but with all these honours bestowed upon him he never regained Barrington which eventually became the property of the Earl of Abergavenny. However the estates did return to the Daubenys when Giles' son Henry married Elizabeth Nevile the Abergavenny heiress.

Henry Daubeny was born in 1494 and later served with Henry VIII who gave him a knighthood in 1509. He supported Henry VIII

1

at the Field of the Cloth of Gold in 1520, when the King met with Francois I of France near Calais. At that time the French King was seeking an alliance against the Emperor Charles V.

Daubeny returned to Somerset to develop his estates, and it was about this time that Barrington Court was begun. The Renaissance had hardly made any impact on building in England at the beginning of the 16th century, yet at Barrington a mansion was built, and although fundamentally of the Gothic style, there is a strong Renaissance flavour. Many of the features found here were not developed in other houses until towards the end of the 16th century. Montacute House, Barrington's near neighbour, is a typical example, and like Montacute it is built of the honey-coloured Ham Hill stone. Daubeny was no stranger to Renaissance architecture, it was already well established in Northern France where he had strong family roots. Daubeny was created Earl of Bridgwater in 1538, and it is almost certain that Barrington Court was far from being completed when he died in 1548.

The house passed to Sir Thomas Arundel, but on being attainted in 1553 it was granted to the Duke of Suffolk who immediately sold to Sir John Clifton. The Cliftons continued to complete the building, making additions to the interior, but debts forced them to sell in 1605 to Sir Thomas Phelips of Montacute. The Strode family of Shepton Mallet were the next owners, William Strode purchased the estates in 1623, and it was his son, another William, who built the brick stable block about 1670, and the Strode family continued to live at Barrington for the next hundred and fifty years.

Daubeny's house surrounded as it was by the formal gardens of that period, created a correct and impressive grandeur, but with the Strode brick additions, they stand less than forty feet to the west and occupy an area almost equal to the main house, Barrington lost some of its scale and regularity characteristic of the early Renaissance.

During the 19th century the fortunes of Barrington Court were in decline. It had many owners after the Strodes, and when in 1907 the National Trust purchased the property, the gardens were overgrown and the house although intact was in a parlous state. This was the first sizeable house to come into possession of the Trust, but it was not until 1920 that any attempt was made to carry out large scale restoration. Even so it was a Colonel A. A. Lyle who completely restored and remodelled the mansion, and made it habitable once more. The interior of Barrington is a reconstruction with panelling and staircases from ruined houses which formed part of Colonel Lyle's collection. It was in order to find a home for this collection that Colonel Lyle obtained a long lease from the National Trust, and set about converting the Strode's brick stable block into a desirable residence where the family still live.

Of the original interior of Barrington nothing remains, but it is most satisfying the way the craftsmanship of bygone woodcarvers slots into Daubeny's construction. The interior of the stable block, which is connected to the main building by a modern passage, contains a number of fine rooms. On the south side is the Wren room where the wainscot from the London house of Sir Christopher Wren adds to the decor.

Barrington Court (17th c. addition)

Berkeley Castle
Gloucestershire

The strikingly handsome Berkeley Castle, the home of the Berkeley family since the middle of the 12th century, stands sentinel beside the Severn estuary. For a thousand years the storms of English history have lashed about its battlements which were built to endure the onslaught of violent times. With its imposing gateway, stout high walls and fortifications everywhere, it is the kind of castle one always conjured up in childhood, where imagination runs riot with men in armour storming its bastions, and defenders twanging their bowstrings through the arrow slits.

Once inside the anguish associated with the exterior is immediately mollified by the tasteful collection of paintings, tapestries, fine furniture and silver, contributions made by earlier generations of Berkeley men and women.

Berkeley was originally an abbey dating probably from the middle of the 8th century, it was then called "Beorc Lea", a Saxon word meaning "birch clearing", and over the years it held considerable power over this part of Wessex. In 910 AD the Danes sailed up the Severn and destroyed the abbey, and so much of its later history has been lost in the mists of time.

About the time of the Norman conquest a young Saxon nobleman of Wessex emerges, and gives his allegiance to the Norman invaders, later to die fighting for William. He left behind him a son Harding, whose grandson, Robert Fitz-Harding was to be the first of the long line of Berkeleys.

Henry Plantagenet of Anjou, later to be Henry II, on arrival in England to claim the throne based himself for a time in Bristol, where his cause received the considerable support of Robert Fitz-Harding, by now one of Bristol's richest merchants. When Henry won the throne his most loyal supporter had to be rewarded, nothing but the best decided the new king, and so the manor and estates, and the lordship of Berkeley was handed over to the Fitz-Hardings. This was in 1153 AD, and the family have held Berkeley till the present day.

Berkeley Castle

Fitz-Harding's occupation of Berkeley was not all that easy, for on moving in he found that the castle was still in possession of Roger de Dursley, but who had recently changed his name to de Berkeley, after giving his support to Henry's opponents. Roger was of course thrown out, and so a dangerous embroilment was created with all the elements of a bitter feud between the two families. Fitz-Harding's sense of compromise finally solved what might have been an intolerable situation, he changed his name to de Berkeley, and married his heir Maurice to Roger's daughter Alicia. To soften the blow further, Robert allowed another son to marry the youngest daughter of the dispossessed Roger, and so Robert Berkeley strengthened the walls of his castle, enjoyed his feudal lordship over the Vale of Berkeley, and founded St. Augustine's Abbey in Bristol, and in due course on his death he was buried there.

It was no easy task for the Berkeleys to hold on to their possessions, these were turbulent times, and survival depended entirely on the side taken when the crown was in dispute. The characteristic quality of the Berkeleys for compromise failed when they betrayed their feudal allegiance to King John. Their future was uncertain, for the unavoidable fate of all feudal traitors was death or the loss of their estates. The Berkeleys were treated lightly by only losing their estates to the Crown, to be restored at a later date by Henry III, but to harmonise this occasion Maurice Berkeley II married the daughter of one of King John's bastards.

But once more the darkening clouds of history were gathering around the turrets of Berkeley Castle. Edward II was deep in trouble

5

with the Lords Ordainers, a baronial committee with powers to restrict the offices of the Crown, and in his humiliation turned to the Despensers (father and son) for advice. Once again a Berkeley chose the wrong side, and Maurice III in joining a revolt against the King paid for it with his life.

Edward's rule with the Despensers was short lived. Edward's Queen Isabella joined forces with her lover Roger Mortimer to get rid of this ill-favoured pair. A plot was hatched and with baronial support the Despensers were hanged, and the King became a fugitive on the run. Now Maurice's son Thomas had married Mortimer's daughter, and with the Queen and Mortimer established in power the Berkeleys once more recovered their lands. The wretched King Edward was eventually brought unceremoniously to Berkeley Castle, where he was incarcerated for five months in the hope that he would soon die. The Queen was growing impatient and gave fresh orders regarding his survival. The King's jailors were Sir John Maltravers and Sir Thomas Gurney, and the Queen's message was not lost on their pitiless minds, and so on the night of the 21st September 1327, Edward, a homosexual, was put to death in the vilest way, and it has been said that the tortured shrieks of the King were even heard outside the castle walls. The King was found later abandoned in his cell, and nausea generated by this catalogue of horror was so intense that the church was compelled to give the King a martyr's burial near the high altar in Gloucester Cathedral.

Quite naturally Thomas Berkeley had to answer some pretty searching questions by Edward III, and he was summoned before Parliament to account for his behaviour, the Berkeley cool once again stood him in good stead, and he came off lightly, restoring his reputation by fighting alongside Edward III at Crecy and Poitiers.

The following years were certainly not without incident, the Berkeley's hold on their lands did not go unchallenged. There was the affair of the powerful de Lisles who were pressing hard in their claims by marriage to the Berkeley estates, and once more the Berkeley cunning showed no lack of ingenuity. Hostilities were finally settled by an ambush in 1469 at Nibley Green, resulting in the death of Lord de Lisle.

In Henry VII's reign the then Lord Berkeley conveyed the castle to the King in return for certain privileges and protection, and only on the death of Edward VI did it finally return to the family. During the Civil War Berkeley was defended for the King, Cromwell's men forced a breach in the curtain wall, and this can still be seen today. On the restoration of Charles II the Berkeley Earldom was created in the person of George Lord Berkeley.

The 18th century sees the saga of the Berkeleys moving into calmer waters, but not without the occasional skeleton revealing itself. This was so with Frederick Augustus, 5th Earl of Berkeley born in 1745. He was something of a gambler and raffish in character, but perhaps he was better known for his seduction of the 17-year-old Mary Coles, daughter of the local butcher. Berkeley had met his match, moving into the castle she completely took over control, running the estate more efficiently than ever before, and at the same time she bore the Earl eight children. Eventually the Earl and Mary married in London, and to prove the legitimacy of some of their children, the Earl was compelled to state before the House of Lords that he had married Mary secretly in 1786, thus began the Berkeley Peerage Case in which the Earl was eventually defeated. Mary Cole was a remarkable woman, after the Earl died, she was proposed to by the Duke of Clarence who lived in Sydney Place, Bath. He became later William IV, and so had she consented Mary could well have been Queen of England.

The Berkeleys still live in the Castle, although the titles have long since disappeared. The present owner is Robert John Berkeley, and so after nearly a thousand years of history the Berkeleys are still in possession.

Blaise Castle Estate and Blaise Hamlet, Henbury, Bristol

In an age of increasing humanity and softening of manners it is difficult to understand how the majority of the people of England lived one hundred and fifty years ago. William Cobbett, a remarkable Englishman, a man of decided views who set out on a mission of wandering and in doing so witnessed the suffering of the hapless farm labourers evicted from their cottages in the great enclosures of the common lands, and the weavers of Somerset and Wiltshire who had lost out to the large mills of Yorkshire. He wrote his "Rural Rides" as a stolid look at wretchedness and as an indictment of the times. But it was not all bad, fine men existed and one such man was a West Country squire, a Quaker and a banker who lived at Blaise Castle House, just outside the village of Henbury near Bristol, his name was John Scandrett Harford.

Harford was concerned for the welfare of the employees who had worked for him and his family on the Blaise Castle Estate, and so he planned a small village, a quiet sanctuary where the old retainers of his family could find security and retire at the end of their working life. Nothing but the best for Squire Harford, and so the architect John Nash, the designer of Regent Street and the terraces surrounding Regent's Park, and the Royal Pavilion at Brighton was consulted. The year was 1811, the Prince of Wales had just become the Prince Regent, and Nash was grappling with the problems of the principles of town-planning and townscape, and now he was called upon to plan a tiny village of only a few cottages dispersed about a village green to include a pillared sundial on a stone pump.

Placed carefully around a lovely green, the cottages all have their own individuality; each one is unusually picturesque and each harmonises with the remaining nine. They have gabled windows, and their tall chimneys are of different designs. Some of the cottages are thatched with verandas and porches, with projections and recessions, and around the outside walls are benches where the occupants can enjoy their leisure hours. This is Nash in his most romantic mood.

Cottages and Pumps, Blaise Hamlet

Nash planned the cottages with imagination and care, creating each so that no front door overlooked that of another cottage, giving each inmate complete privacy. Round the edge of the green is a pathway, and in the centre is a tall pump which is now no longer in use, but bears an inscription which tells the story of the hamlet's origins.

Entering the little lane through a copse of trees you are led into a different world, quietly remote from the busy suburban roads of Henbury, in fact unless you know what you are looking for, Blaise Hamlet could be so easily missed; from outside there is little to see, but once inside you are rewarded with a great sense of isolation and peace. For nearly thirty years now the hamlet has been owned by the National Trust, and under its careful stewardship the cottages have been maintained in almost pristine condition.

Nearby is the Blaise Castle Estate which takes its name from the Chapel of St. Blaise which stood originally on the site of the present "Castle". Between the 16th and 17th centuries the manor of Henbury was held by the Sadleir family, then in 1653 one Edward Capell, a Bristol merchant, leased the manor house from Sir Ralph Sadleir and continued to live at Blaise until 1687. The property came into the hands of Thomas Farr, Master of the Society of Merchant Venturers, at the beginning of the 18th century and with the help of the architect Robert Mylne, Farr built his castle in 1771.

9

Cottages, Blaise Hamlet

Farr suffered considerable financial losses in Bristol, and the Castle came on the market for sale to be purchased eventually by John Scandrett Harford in 1789. A few years later the old manor house was demolished, and Harford built the present house and laid out the parkland. The Harford family remained at Blaise until 1926 when the estate was purchased by the Bristol Corporation, which included the "Castle" for an amount just under £20000.

Harford engaged William Paty to design the house, and Humphry Repton to landscape the parkland. Work was commenced in 1795 and the house was finished a year later. The interior of the house now contains the Folk Museum section of the Bristol City Museum. John Nash built the little thatched dairy opposite the conservatory in 1802, and this delightful building together with an 18th century corn mill from West Harptree has been preserved as part of the museum.

Blaise Castle Estate is put to many uses during the summer months, but the buildings of Paty and Nash remain, Repton's grand scheme for the landscaping still show his outstanding qualities, and Farr's "folly", the "Castle", has now been restored.

Brympton d'Evercy
Near Yeovil, Somerset

The first time I saw Brympton d'Evercy was in the early days of the Second World War. I was on a training exercise from nearby Lufton Barracks, and had stopped for a break on a slight incline overlooking the parkland surrounding the mansion. From that distance it looked a charming house, and I can recall speculating on the people living there. I had to wait until 1965 for the opportunity of seeing the house at close quarters, and I was not entirely disappointed. At that time it was being used as a school, and looked rather shabby and neglected, and yet it must have appealed, because in an article I was writing I said "A short drive brings you to the entrance gates of the school, although there is a notice saying that the drive was a private road, there is a right of way to the church. The drive is through wooded parkland, and on emerging into the open you are confronted by an incomparable group of Hamstone buildings". It was ten years later I paid my second visit and met the present owners Mr. and Mrs. Charles Clive-Ponsonby-Fane, they prefer to be called Mr. and Mrs. Clive, who had recently opened their part 16th century and part 17th century house to visitors.

Brympton d'Evercy, lost in a labyrinth of quiet lanes, is only a short distance from its better known neighbour, Montacute House, and can be reached after leaving Yeovil on the A3088 road, which also leads to Montacute. The estate is the historic seat of the d'Evercy and Sydenham families, and since 1731 the home of the Ponsonby-Fane family. Its history stretches back 750 years, since the early 13th century, when the land was purchased by the d'Evercy family. They were responsible for building much of the parish church which stands hard by, and for building the Priest House alongside. The estate remained in this family until purchased by the well known John Stourton as a dowry for his daughter when she married John Sydenham.

Each generation of the wealthy Sydenham family added to the manor house. The West Front is built in the Tudor style, with the coat of arms of Henry VIII occupying a position north of the turret stair-

Brympton d'Evercy

case, and here I quote from the official guidebook 'It may appear un-
usual for a country squire to emblazon the front of his house with the
Royal Arms, but this is not the pretentious gesture it may seem. The
Sydenhams were fully entitled to this honour as a result of ties with
the Blood Royal, through marrying into the Stourton family."

The highlight of the mansion is the South Front which overlooks a
fine lake. It has also been the subject of an architectural jangle regarding its architect. This front was certainly commissioned by Sir John
Posthumous Sydenham – the middle name shows that he inherited
from a father dead before he himself was born – and because his second wife, Mary, was a grand-daughter of the 4th Earl of Pembroke,
the same Earl who commissioned Inigo Jones to rebuild Wilton after
its disastrous fire in 1647, it has been assumed that this great
architect, one time Surveyor – General to Charles I, and disciple of
Andrea Palladio, was responsible for the South Front. This line of
thought can be dimissed immediately, Jones died in 1652, whereas the
building of the garden front was commissioned some years later,
about 1678. Furthermore knowing Jones devotion to the disciplines of
Palladianism, it is inconceivable that he could have designed an elevation where the window line commences at one end of the house with a
rounded pediment and terminating the row with a pointed one. If not
Jones, was the design the work of one of his acolytes?

In 1731, about 40 years after the death of Sir John Sydenham, the
estate, heavily in debt, came on the market for sale, and was purchased
by one Francis Fane, a prosperous barrister and member of Parliament. He lived at Brympton for 26 years. On his death, the estates

and mansion were left to his younger brother Thomas, who eventually became the 8th Earl of Westmoreland. The story of the Fanes connection with Brympton really starts from the period when John Fane the 10th Earl owned the property. His first marriage was with Sarah Child, a union very much disapproved of by her father. Although out of favour with his father-in-law, he was much in favour with his king. At various intervals he was Postmaster General, Lord Privy Seal, and Viceroy of Ireland. Whilst holding this office the daughter of his second marriage, Lady Georgiana Fane, fell in love with Arthur Wellesley, aide de camp to the Viceroy, and the future victor of Waterloo. When the young Wellesley asked for her hand in marriage the Viceroy refused, purely on the grounds that he considered the social position of the young soldier was inferior to that of his daughter.

Georgiana and her mother decided to reside at Brympton where they lived together until the Countess died in 1857, and Georgiana continued to manage the running of the estate. She died in 1875 leaving the estate, which was again heavily in debt to her godson Spencer Ponsonby. On inheriting Brympton he assumed the name of Spencer Ponsonby-Fane, and went on to become Private Secretary to Lord Palmerston, and later to become Comptroller of the Lord Chamberlain's Office. He died in 1915, and his eldest son John, who suffered from indifferent health died within a year after inheriting the property, leaving behind two children Richard and Violet. Richard travelled abroad, spending much of his time in Japan, and Violet,

Brympton d'Evercy

she married a Mr. Edward Clive. It was their son Nicholas Clive who inherited Brympton on the death of his uncle, and assumed the additional name Ponsonby-Fane. The upkeep of Brympton was becoming too expensive and so it was decided to move into the rectory behind the stables, and let the house and parkland to a school. The present owner Mr. Clive inherited the estate in 1967. He was concerned for the preservation of this splendid house, and so in July 1974 he regained possession from the school.

Mention must be made of the nearby church. St. Andrews was built during the 14th and 15th centuries, and perhaps because of its isolation it came through the Victorian era almost unscathed, remaining the church of the manor that nobody has ever bothered to meddle with. There are monuments to the d'Evercys, and one to a lady of the 15th century with two small dogs at her feet. Dividing the chapel from the chancel is the tomb of John Sydenham. There is also a delightful 15th century stone screen which bears the arms of John Stourton. The most delightful feature of this little church is the top-heavy bellcote.

The Priest House or dower house has a charming turret and a carved stone fireplace nearly 400 years old. It is interesting to see that the present owners have converted this fine old building into an agricultural museum, which they have packed with the fragments of English rural life. It contains all manner of farming bygones, and Mr. Clive hopes to expand the museum as widely and quickly as possible.

Claverton Manor
(The American Museum)
Near Bath

It has been said that American history began in the West Country, and on studying the facts there would seem to be some substance in this piece of braggadocio. John Cabot sailed from Bristol in 1497 to discover the North American continent, Sir Humphrey Gilbert of Compton Castle in South Devon, founded the first English colony in North America at St. John's Newfoundland in 1583. There was of course Sir Walter Raleigh of Hayes Barton near East Budleigh, and Sir Richard Grenville who hailed from Bideford, the famed seadogs, Hawkins, Drake, and the rest, who were little better than pirates, and of course the Pilgrim Fathers who sailed from Plymouth in 1620. Therefore it is not surprising that an American Folk Museum, the only one of its type outside the USA should be created in the West Country just a few miles from Bath. In fact the delightful countryside of Claverton Down is host to an imaginative enterprise to reconstruct the American way of life through to the mid-nineteenth century, and so, a once stately English home, the scene of that great Americanophile Winston Churchill's first political speech in 1897, now presents the essence of many early American homes. Claverton Manor and its parkland is to all intents and purposes an outpost of the United States of America in those early pioneering colonial days.

The present manor house dates from 1820, and was built to designs by Sir Jeffry Wyatville, brother of James Wyatt, architect to George IV, and who remodelled parts of Chatsworth House for the 6th Duke of Devonshire. His style at Claverton is severe, but he had the satisfaction of building higher up the hillside overlooking the old 16th century mansion, on an eminence giving noble views of the Avon valley. The east front consists of two rounded bays at each end with a centre porch supporting Ionic columns, but the south front presents the best architectural composition consisting of five bays in three storeys divided by four Ionic pilasters which support a plain pediment.

The first manor or Court-house was built by Bishop Ralf de

Claverton Manor

Salopia about the year 1340. This prelate was one of the most munificent of the early bishops. He built the Vicars close and some of the choristers houses at Wells, as well as the church at Winscombe. The Claverton estate managed to escape the fate of other ecclesiastical manors at the Dissolution, but it was sold eventually to the wealthy Matthew Colthurst, who figures so largely in the purchase of monastic property during the 16th century in the area around Bath. Colthurst's son Edmund inherited the manor and sold to Edward Hungerford who built the Tudor mansion in 1588. Of this house only the gateposts and terraces remain, the Regency mansion being built higher up the hillside.

The Tudor mansion passed next to Sir William Bassett towards the end of the 16th century, and his occupation of the manor is recalled in the nearby church where the chancel contains a monument dedicated to Sir William and his wife, and dated 1613. There is an interesting story concerning the manor during the Civil War. My lord was entertaining a party of friends loyal to the King's cause, when suddenly an uncomfortable brouhaha in the matter of a cannonball, directed from across the other side of the valley shattered the wall of the manor narrowly missing the guests as they sat at dinner. There had been a small engagement near the ferry between a patrol of Roundhead soldiers and local Royalist troops. The shot was intended by the Roundhead gunners as a warning to the villagers not to interfere with their advance.

16

A local landowner by the name of William Skrine purchased in 1714 and later sold to Ralph Allen of Bath, but during the break up of the Allen estates after his death the manor reverted to the Skrines once more. It was a John Vivian, an amateur architect who pulled this mansion down, and during the building of the new house he was constantly at loggerheads with Wyatville over the design, and he found that the building on completion lacked the kitchens.

Nearly 100000 visitors are attracted to the Museum every year, they come to taste Mary Washington's gingerbread baked in an 18th century oven from a recipe found in an old worn cookery book. They like to linger in the herb shop, or the New England Country Store where one may be forgiven in thinking that one may have momentarily strayed on to a "Western" film set. One delightful touch is the Conestoga covered wagon, a former "Prairie Schooner", which conveyed those early pioneers across the American continent, and which is so well recorded on our television screens today.

The highlight of the Museum is the reproduction of George Washington's garden at Mount Vernon, Virginia, in the English countryside, a gift to Claverton by the Colonial Dames of America. The garden is in a secluded corner of the parkland, well below the level of the house, and surrounded by a white fence. It is approached by descending a steep flight of steps along sloping lawns. Once inside the enclosure the layout of the garden is most attractive, the flower beds are well planted and a delight to wander among. Not to be missed, although tucked away in a far corner, is a duplicate of the tiny octagonal garden house, furnished as a schoolroom where Washington taught his grand-children.

Claverton Manor gardens

Clevedon Court
Near Clevedon, Avon

Though there are remains of an earlier·building, possibly 13th century, much of Clevedon Court as seen today dates from the early 14th century, and is one of the very few complete houses of its period that has survived the ravages of time. It is unquestionably one of the most beautiful and interesting of medieval houses displaying a simple, but correctness of style.

The Court lies beneath Court Hill, overlooking Nailsea Moor and the intrusion of the M5 motorway. The moor is an area of low lying ground, much of which lies below high water mark, and is protected by a sea wall running almost the whole way from Clevedon to Woodspring Priory, north of Weston-super-Mare. Contrary to the usual custom of manor house and church to be next door to one another, the late 13th century parish church of St. Andrew is built nearly two miles west of the Court in the old village and harbour of Clevedon Pill, which seems to suggest that at one time church and manor were cut off from each other during the high tides of winter, making the existing packhorse roads impassable. Clevedon Court may well stand where it does so that the de Clevedons, the original owners and builders of the Court, could always be within dry shod of reaching Bristol, whence almost everything had to be brought to Clevedon by packhorse till the middle of the 18th century by which time the Bristol coaching road was constructed to give Bristolians access to the town of Clevedon.

The de Clevedon family acquired the manor during the reign of Henry II. Henry Plantagenet had installed himself in Bristol where he received considerable assistance from the many wealthy merchants, self seeking and looking for further loot to plunder they supported his claim to the throne of England.

It was Sir John de Clevedon who in 1320 commenced building the present manor house. He died in 1336 leaving the Court to his son Edmund, who died without any heirs in 1376. The estates passed to the Wake family who held Clevedon until the reign of Charles I. It was

Clevedon Court

John Wake who succeeded to Clevedon in 1558, and it was he who built the west end of the house and much of the Tudor additions. In 1630 Sir Baldwin Wake sold the manor to John Digby, first Earl of Bristol, and on the death of the third Earl the estate was purchased in 1709 by Abraham Elton, a wealthy Bristol merchant, and a man of considerable skills and achievements.

Elton was master of the Merchant Venturers Company and one time Mayor of Bristol. In 1716 he was created High Sheriff of Gloucestershire, and in the next year was made a Baronet for services to the House of Hanover. His many interests in shipping would have connected him with the slave trade that brought so much wealth into the port of Bristol during that period. From 1722 until his death in 1728 he was Member of Parliament for Bristol. Elton was without doubt the first of his line who gained success by their scholarship as members of parliament, inventors, writers, and patrons of the arts, and Clevedon Court became the venue for the men of letters of the time, attaining a large measure of literary fame.

Abraham Elton, the second Baronet, followed his father in all his public offices, with equal success, but his eldest son, the third Baronet was a profligate who did his best to spend the wealth accummulated by his grandfather, and who died a bankrupt in France. The second son who succeeded as the fourth Baronet rebuilt the West wing in Strawberry Hill Gothick soon after he inherited the property in 1761, using the same architect who built Arnos Court on the Bath side of Bristol. Later members of the family considered this front entirely out of sympathy with the character of the Court, and in 1862 Sir Arthur Hallam Elton removed the West front and rebuilt in the Elizabethan style to the designs of Charles Davis, Bath City Architect. A disastrous fire in 1882 destroyed a large portion of the West front, but it was rebuilt to plans designed once more by Davis.

The fifth Baronet, the Reverend Sir Abraham Elton succeeded in 1790. He was a clergyman and a fanatical anti-Methodist, he would roam the countryside like some 18th century Savonarola crying out against the perversion of the church. He took little interest in the Court, preferring to live in Bristol. It was his second wife Mary Stewart, referred to some times as "Old Lady Elton" whom he married in 1825 when he was seventy, who played such an important role in altering the Court, devoting much time in cluttering the interior with mock Tudor additions.

Sir Charles Abraham Elton, the sixth Baronet, became a Unitarian to the disgust of his father, and to add further fuel to his father's discontent he ran away with Sarah Smith, daughter of a Bristol merchant. Hearing of the marriage the reverend gentleman rode post haste to Bristol to stop the ceremony, however both became reconciled later with Sir Abraham, and on his death in 1842 Sir Charles succeeded to the estates.

Sir Charles was a great classical scholar, and a gifted poet. He had many literary associates, and Clevedon Court became the Valhalla of the literati. Coleridge lived in a cottage nearby, and Tennyson, Charles Lamb, Robert Southey, and Thackeray were frequent visitors. Clevedon Court was the inspiration for "Castlewood" in Thackeray's celebrated novel "Henry Esmond", and again in "Vanity Fair", Thackeray's Amelia is drawn from Jane Brookfield, Sir Charles' daughter.

Sir Arthur Hallam Elton succeeded Sir Charles in 1853, and like his family before him, he was a man of many talents. He became Member of Parliament for Bath in 1857, but resigned two years later to show his opposition to the Crimean War, he died in 1884, and the title passed to his nephew, Sir Edmund Harry Elton. Here began a new slant to this erudite family, for Sir Edmund became the potter of the family, and introduced the now famous Elton Ware pottery, characterised by its brilliant metallic crackle – glaze.

Sir Arthur Elton was the last member of the family to own Clevedon. With increasing costs for repairs, combined with death duties, Sir Arthur found the burden too heavy, and so in 1961 and with the assistance of the Society for the Protection of Ancient Buildings, arrangements were made for the property to be taken over by the National Trust, and considerable restoration was then carried out.

There were many difficulties facing David Nye the architect appointed for the re-modelling. The problem was how to deal with the remains of Sir John Wake's West wing, reconstructed three times, and in the process losing much of the original work with the exception of the lower part of the south gable. The problems were overcome, and it is now almost possible to see Clevedon Court as John Wake must have seen it in 1570.

The terrace gardens are noted for the rare plants which grow there and a magnificent London plane tree and a mulberry just below the house may have been planted by Abraham Elton, the Bristol merchant, nearly 270 years ago.

Corsham Court
Corsham, Wilts.

The Methuens or Methvens, originally of German extraction, settled in Scotland nearly 800 years ago, and gave considerable service to Malcolm III, King of Scotland, who bestowed upon the first Methuen the Barony of Perthshire. It was during the persecution of the protestants in Scotland that the brothers John and Andrew de Methven, both of whom took a permanent part in zealously promoting the Reformation, fearing reprisals, fled to England and were well received by Queen Elizabeth. John's son Paul was particularly favoured in receiving a stall in Wells Cathedral, and other preferments in Somerset, to become later chaplain to John Still, Bishop of Bath and Wells. In this capacity he married a wealthy Somerset heiress and become possessed of property at Bradford-on-Avon. The eldest son of this union was Paul Methwin — notice the spelling of the name has changed once more — from whom descends the present family of Methuen of Corsham Court.

Paul married Grace Ashe daughter of a wealthy clothier of Bradford-on-Avon, and he eventually took over the burgeoning cloth mills of his father-in-law, and amassed a large fortune. Up to now the cloth made at Bradford was of the coarse kind, but Methwin had seen the processes which produced the fine material from Flanders and Florence. So conscious of the inferiority of his own cloth production, he took advantage of the many Huguenots at that time fleeing from religious persecution in France and Holland and coming to England. Many of these refugees were weavers and Methwin knowing of their skills invited them to settle in Bradford where they were employed by Methwin in his own mills, and so in this way he learned the secrets of the manufacture of the finer cloth which came from the continent. This importation of foreign labour was far from welcomed by the townspeople, and the town's officials imposed an indemnity of £100 on Paul Methwin lest these weavers should become a liability on the inhabitants of Bradford.

Paul's eldest son John who preferred to spell his name Methven,

Corsham Court

was a person of some outstanding ability, who became Lord Chancellor of Ireland, and represented Devizes in five Parliaments. There was turmoil in Ireland and he failed to assuage the Irish Parliament, and finally left Ireland in despair in 1701, returning to England where he achieved greater success. For in 1703 he concluded a treaty with Portugal whereby the cloth from England was to be allowed into Portugal, and in return certain privileges were allowed in favour of that country's wines, in particular the importation of port which gradually replaced Burgundy which had hitherto been the popular wine drunk in England. John Methven has been described as a "profligate rogue without religion or morals, but cunning enough", and on another occasion he was referred to as "a man of intrigue very muddly in his conceptions".

One of his sons was killed in a brawl abroad in 1694, but the other who became Sir Paul Methuen was the most distinguished. For many years he was ambassador to Spain, and then in 1706 he was appointed a Lord of the Admiralty, and after holding further important offices of state he was promoted in 1725 to the Office of Treasurer of the Household. Methuen was an avid reader, and on being asked on one occasion by Queen Caroline what he had been reading, riposted "I have been reading a poor book on a poor subject, the Kings and Queens of England".

Sir Paul who died in 1757 had formed a great collection of pictures during his many travels overseas, and having no children be bequeathed his entire collection to his cousin another Paul with a request that the paintings were to be found a worthy home. So in

23

1745 Paul Methuen purchased Corsham Court and remodelled the mansion to receive the Methuen Collection of pictures and objets d'art.

Corsham Court estates originally belonged to the King, and then later became part of the dower of the Queens of England. In 1582 the estates were sold to Thomas Smythe – "Customer" Smythe as he was called because of his fiddling the customs dues collected in London. He built a Tudor house with gables and mullioned windows, much of which remains today.

In 1602 Corsham Court became the property of the Hungerford family of Farleigh Castle, and then after passing through a number of families it was purchased by Paul Methuen. It was decided to retain as much of the Elizabethan character of the south front and to rebuild the north side as a new entrance front in the classical style. Nathaniel Ireson of Wincanton, who was engaged to carry out Colen Campbell's plans at Stourhead, supplied designs for Corsham. Much of Ireson's work was multilated later by Capability Brown, better skilled as a landscape gardener than as an architect. Brown built what was virtually a completely new east front outside the original building in order to form the picture gallery. Since that period a series of architects have had a hand in the remodelling of Corsham Court.

Paul Cobb Methuen succeeded his father in 1795 and he employed Humphrey Repton and John Nash to alter the east front. Nash rebuilt the north front in the Gothick style, and replanned the interior to provide a great hall running the whole length of the original Elizabethan house. Paul Cobb Methuen died in 1816 and was followed by his son, who later became the first Baron Methuen.

Now Lord Methuen was dissatisfied with Nash's treatment of the north front, so Charles Bellamy was employed to rebuild the north side in the 19th century pseudo Tudor, and much of Nash's interior was reconstructed to provide for a grand new staircase.

The third Lord Methuen was the field marshal who was heavily defeated at Magersfontein during the Boer War, but distinguished himself later when Lord Roberts became commander-in-chief. He died in 1932 and his son the late Lord Methuen inherited the mansion and its beautiful parkland. He was a talented painter, to become later President of the Royal West of England Academy, and an associate of the Royal Academy. Under his influence the Bath Academy of Art came to Corsham Court, which is not surprising for the picture gallery is perhaps the dominating feature of Corsham Court, retaining much of the original decor and the furniture that was originally made for it. The collection includes paintings by Van Dyck, Reynolds, Jansen, Lely, Kneller, Gainsborough, Romney and others.

A reminder of the religious intolerance of the 16th and 17th centuries is provided in the return to the parish church, which stands hard by the entrance to the park at Corsham, of the original royal coat of arms of William and Mary. It was an artistic feature of the church from 1693 until its removal to Corsham Court in the 19th century. Beautifully painted on a wooden panel about four feet square, the coat of arms was discovered stored in a room at the Court. It had been restored by the late Lord Methuen who considered it to be the property of the vicar and that it should be returned to the church.

Henry VIII is often regarded as the arch enemy of monastic institutions, but it was his son Edward VI who ordered the removal of the rood screens as symbols of Rome, and their replacement by the royal coat of arms. Little is known of the origin of the Corsham coat of arms, but it is thought that it was "An expression of loyalty by the parishioners to the new king after James II had been booted out of the country".

Dodington House
Near Bath

Never before have so many great houses in Britain been open to the public, never have stately houses attracted so many visitors, and yet, many people would say, never have so many of them been so seriously threatened. The danger is not from insensitive owners who have little regard for conservation and preservation, but from the lack of financial resources necessary to stop decay which age inevitably dictates. The National Trust has done much to allay the dangers of any future destruction, and many fine mansions have been preserved for posterity, but in the majority of cases the role they play today is that of a museum. Dodington however still remains a family home, and has been just that to the Codringtons since Elizabethan times. The Tudor house was built in 1560 by Thomas Weekes who sold it to Giles Codrington soon after it was completed. It was a fine gabled house situated among well landscaped parkland.

The early history of the Codringtons seem to be centred on the parish of Wapley, a mile or so west of the present house, where they appear to have been minor landowners. It was John Codrington who brought some prominence to the family, he was born in 1364, and at the age of 50 accompanied Henry V to France, and was present at the siege of Harfleur suffering terrible privation in the run up to the Battle of Agincourt. After the victory, and as a reward for his personal successes in the field, he was appointed standard bearer to the king. He finally retired to Wapley and his tomb can be seen in Wapley parish church.

Christopher Codrington imigrated to Barbados in the reign of Charles I, and under pioneering conditions, developing virgin land he built the foundations of his vast fortune, which was further enhanced by marrying the sister of the wealthy Sir James Drax. His son, the second Christopher, was born in 1640, and as a young man he amassed one of the largest individual fortunes in the West Indies by careful management of his sugar plantations, and savoured success in the political field by driving the French out of the Leeward Islands, to

WOOD

WILTSHIRE/AVON BORDER

M4 Junction 18 one mile.

DODINGTON PARK ESTATE

One of England's historic stately homes in a magnificent parkland setting.

The seat of the Codrington family.

DODINGTON, JAMES WYATT'S LAST GREAT CLASSICAL HOUSE

With suite of 7 fine reception rooms,

12 bedrooms and 6 bathrooms,

domestic offices, extensive basement. (Roof recently renovated).

The Dower House (let)

Home Farm House (let). Farm Buildings.

Stable block with 3 flats, stabling and garaging

2 Cottages (subject to Life Tenancies)

Formal gardens and parkland by Capability Brown, with 2 lakes, woodland and paddocks

About 157 Acres

23 Berkeley Square, London W1X 6AL. Tel. 01-629 9050. Telex 21242

Dodington House

become their Governor in 1698. But even the fortunes of a sugar king like Codrington was not proof against the intrigues and political persecution in Barbados, and so he returned to Antigua and continued to develop his estates there. The family continued to retain large interests in the West Indies until well into the early part of the present century.

The third Christopher, son of the second Christopher, came to be regarded as the most outstanding member of the Codringtons, intellectually he was quite brilliant, possessing considerable charm and force of character. He was born in 1668, and educated at All Souls Oxford. After campaigning in Flanders with considerable success he returned to the Leeward Islands in 1699 as Captain-General under William III, but political quarrels cut short his Governorship, and compelled him to return to the Codrington estates in Antigua where he died of fever in 1710 leaving no heirs. His body was brought to Oxford and buried in All Souls Chapel. He left a legacy of £10000 to the college to found the Codrington Library, which is second only to the Bodleian Library, and at the same time under the terms of his will his large and comprehensive book collection was also donated.

It was left to Christopher Bethell Codrington a later descendant to rebuild the house completely. He commissioned James Wyatt, a man of lethargic disposition, who did not mind whether he was required to build in the Classical or Gothic styles, as a matter of principle he preferred the Gothic. He despised the work of Robert Adam and remarked on returning from Italy in 1804, "I found the public taste corrupted by the Adams and I was obliged to comply with it". Perhaps it

27

was fortunate that his patron preferred the Classical style for his new house and followed the ritual of many of his contemporaries by pulling down an older building and replacing it with the Palladian orders.

The exterior of the new house is austere, almost to the point of starkness, and in many ways pedestrian when it is compared with the lavish style of the interior. A great portico of six Corinthian columns, reaching from pediment to ground-level without any supporting base dominates the West entrance front, leaving room for a carriage to draw up to the front door, the whole would appear to be out of proportion with the remainder.

The South front which displays a far better style of mathematical correctness, consists of a recessed centre, with Corinthian pilasters supporting a rectangular pediment flanked by balustrades. The East front has a bow at each end with a plain centre, and the whole for effect relies on the backdrop of the splendid parkland, landscaped by Capability Brown, which is the most important ingredient of Dodington.

Wyatt's skills were reserved for the interior, where his concentration on the central staircase has paid off. It rises in double flights from the inner hall, surrounded by an arcade of fluted Corinthian columns, which in turn supports a further series of pillars on the first floor. The ironwork in the staircase is of particularly fine craftsmanship, and came from the Georgian mansion at Fonthill in Wiltshire, which at the time was being demolished by William Beckford who had already commissioned Wyatt to build his ill-fated abbey on the site.

West Entrance Front, Dodington House

The principal rooms have considerable charm, and bear the stamp of family pride. Doorcases and fireplaces are restrained in design, but the doors of veneered mahogany display punctilious elegance. There is no doubt that the most magnificent of these are those to be seen in the Drawing Room, a splendid room in many ways, well proportioned, with large windows providing fine views over the gardens and park.

Dodington has two entrance lodges, one leads to the Chipping Sodbury road and consists of an arched gateway surmounted by the Codrington coat of arms, with an adjoining lodge. The other lodge which is on the A46 (Bath to Stroud road) is located only a few yards from the M4 motorway junction 18. This is now the main entrance to the house. The lodge here is in the form of a rotunda, and the drive from here is over two miles to the mansion and takes the visitor down through beautiful woodland into a valley where house, lakes, and gardens present a matchless scene.

There is one tragic note in the building of Dodington, James Wyatt and Christopher Bethell Codrington were travelling back from Gloucestershire to London on the 14th September 1813 after inspecting the house which was now almost completed. Driving in one of the family's coaches they collided with a post-chaise travelling at a high speed near Marlborough. The coach overturned killing Wyatt, whilst Codrington received only minor injuries.

The present owner, Major Simon Codrington who lives on the estate with his family, has done much to make his home interesting and accessible. For the seeker of outdoors entertainment Dodington has much to offer, the Carriage Museum is one of the largest in the south of England, and is housed in the large Stable Block built by Wyatt. It contains a collection of over 30 coaches, and if a mailcoach jaunt around the park is required, it is possible to lay this on. For the quiet walker, Dodington Park can offer a series of trails alongside the lake, or through its delightful woodland.

29

Dyrham Park
Near Bath

William Blathwayt was the son of a lawyer who entered the diplomatic service, serving under no less than four monarchs – from Charles II to Queen Anne – receiving in 1683 the appointment of Secretary of War, a post he continued to hold until 1704. For quite a considerable time he represented Bath in Parliament, and was prominent in public affairs under William III as a Whig. All this made Blathwayt an extremely important and wealthy man, thus at the height of his career, and following the traditions of the great land-owners of that period, he began to rebuild the Tudor mansion at Dyrham which he had inherited through his wife Mary, daughter and heiress of John Wynter, whom he had married at Dyrham Parish Church on Christmas Eve 1686.

The Wynters originated from Lydney, bordering on the Forest of Dean, and it was a George Wynter, brother of Admiral Sir William Wynter who was prominent in defeating the Spanish Armada, who first acquired the Tudor mansion. A family romance surrounds William Blathwayt's courtship of Mary Wynter. Apparently in the offing there was another suiter for the hand of Mary, a country squire living south of Bath. During a visit of this young man to Dyrham he met Blathwayt who had already achieved considerable success at Court, and it was not long before the squire suspected that the courtier found more favour in the eyes of the all important Mary than he did. Seeking an opportunity to put an end to his affair, the young squire managed to shoot Blathwayt through the hand during a hunting trip in the parkland. The occurrence passed off lightly, although at one stage the fur started to fly, and as a result the squire was no longer welcomed at Dyrham.

It was after the death of his wife in 1691 that William Blathwayt began to rebuild the older house of the Wynters. A relatively unknown French architect by the name of Hauduroy was commissioned to design the West front, and work was commenced in 1692. The design is simple and correct, and considered by many to be the most

West Front, Dyrham Park

inspiring of the two fronts. There are two rows of windows, fifteen on the first floor with the projecting ends accounting for three each. A balustrade runs the length of the parapet interrupted by urns and with a central figure of Hermes. Quite a splendid setting on a terrace flanked by pavilions and the historic church nestling beside it looking out across a long level of lawn to the plain below.

Blathwayt's partnership with Hauduroy was short lived. In 1694 William Talman was working at Chatsworth House for the Duke of Devonshire, and his burgeoning success as an architect persuaded Blathwayt to engage him to design the East front. Talman's front broken by a slight projection at each end consists of two principal storeys with an attic floor surmounted by a balustrade, with an eagle holding the Blathwayt coat of arms. The two upper floors contain thirteen windows each, and there are six on each side of the entrance door. The whole is flanked by the orangery at the south end and a balancing arcade on the north which runs into the hillside.

For all his shrewdness as a capable administrator and an able Government official, Blathwayt became a patron of the arts and in many ways appeared to have been something of a dilettante. He made many visits to Holland mostly in connection with business of state, so it is not surprising that the house contains many Dutch paintings, the walls of the Vestibule are covered with embossed gilt leather hangings which Blathwayt obtained in the Hague. Among the paintings there is a much-admired picture by Van Hoogstraeten, painted in 1662 and entitled "View Down a Corridor". The bird paintings by Hondecoeter and the beautiful pieces of blue and white Delftware all show

31

Blathwayt the collector. The decor of the interior reflects the Blathwayt connection with the American Plantations. From here he was able to obtain the cedarwood for one of the staircases and Virginian walnut to panel the Diogenes Room.

The Drawing Room not only displays the elegant furniture made specially by Linnel for William Blathwayt's grandson, but it also contains two of Dyrham's most valued pictures. One by Murillo is entitled "Peasant Woman and Boy", and on the opposite wall hangs an identical painting by Gainsborough and painted in 1760. It is said that the third William Blathwayt so admired the original owned by his uncle that he persuaded Gainsborough to paint him a replica for his own home. However sometime later, perhaps by inheritance, the original also came to Dyrham.

During the late 17th century and early 18th century the Dutch Garden was much in vogue, and knowing the Blathwayt's meticulous attention to detail the formality of this style made its appeal, and so a large part of the estate was laid out with terraces, parterres, and a canal with fountains and a cascade, similar in many ways to the restored Dutch Gardens at Westbury Court at Westbury on Severn and now belonging to the National Trust. Later in the 18th century landscape architects like Capability Brown, William Kent, and Humphrey Repton were changing the formality of the Dutch Gardens. By now the style was planned to site a house in an artifically constructed landscape by vistas, water, trees and Greek temples and statues. The parkland as seen today is mostly the work of Humphrey Repton who started the alterations in the early 19th century, and now cushions this elegant house within the folds of its hills.

The Blathwayts remained in possession of Dyrham until 1956, when house and contents were sold to the Ministry of Works, who transferred them to the National Trust. Only recently the parkland which was never included in the original transfer has now been purchased by the Trust.

Great Chalfield Manor
Near Bradford-on-Avon, Wilts.

Tucked away down typically narrow West Country lanes stands a cluster of buildings which is Great Chalfield Manor. Although its shell dates from the 14th century, all the main features are of the 15th century, and have remained substantially unaltered since then.

Recorded history of the Manor goes back to the time of "Domesday", and later records show the Manor in the ownership of the Percys, a branch of the family of de Percy who came to England with William the Conqueror and fought at Hastings alongside the many other rapacious adventurers who crossed the Channel in 1066 in fulfilment of the many promises made to them by William in return for their loyalty. Fortunately for posterity the history of the early owners has been recorded in a manuscript known as the Tropenell Cartulary which was commenced by Thomas Tropenell in 1464 and is shewn today to visitors to the Manor.

A granddaughter of Sir Harry de Percy married in the early 13th century a Walter Tropenell of Sopworth near Badminton, thus commencing the long line of the Tropenell's occupation of Chalfield. But credit must be given to Thomas Tropenell, a wealthy merchant and at one time M.P. for Bath, for transforming the building and the site which was originally chosen for defensive rather than for architectural reasons, into a fine manor house containing a delightful blending of old and new, the results of careful planning by the 15th century builder.

Thomas was succeeded by his son Christopher, but in the 16th century the heiress Anne, the last of Tropenells, married John Eyre of Wedhampton, whose family originated from Derbyshire, and later developed strong ties in Wiltshire. John's son William inherited the estates on the death of his father in 1581. He became M.P. for Wiltshire and later knighted for his services to the County. He had three wives and eleven children, and on his death there was considerable confusion regarding the disposal of the estate, but it finally passed to Sir John who sold the property in 1630 to Sir Richard Gurney. In the late

The North Front, Great Chalfield Manor

17th century the Halls of Bradford-on-Avon were the owners, and it was to John Hall's grand-daughter, Rachael Baynton, that the estate passed next. Rachael in the meantime had married the first Duke of Kingston, and so on his death the property passed to the second and last Duke of Kingston who married the notorious already wedded Elizabeth Chudleigh, and whose bigamy trial before the House of Lords in 1776 was a social event of the first magnitude. The Duke sold the house in 1770 to Robert Neale of Shaw House, Melksham, and so ended the lengthy series of owners, all of which had some family connection with each other.

Robert Neale's daughter married Admiral Sir Henry Burrard, who adopted the name of Beale on inheriting Chalfield. The Manor then passed to the widow of the Admiral's brother who sold in 1878 to Mr. G. P. Fuller of Neston, and in 1912 it passed by purchase to Major R. F. Fuller, and from him the National Trust have become the owners since 1943.

Chalfield is a compact little place with the green countryside of Wiltshire pressing closely in on all sides. In that uncertain period of the Peasant's Revolt of 1381 it was necessary for many houses to have some means of defence, and the builders of Chalfield had this in mind when constructing the moat, which would have given considerable peace of mind to those early occupiers. It is all very innocuous today for the moat is only a fraction of its original size, and much shallower. Its banks are now fringed by reeds and willows whose reflections nod quietly in the water. To enter the outer court you pass over the moat and through the gatehouse, ahead is the west wing con-

Archway leading to forecourt, Great Chalfield Manor

taining an arched gateway leading into the forecourt, and to the main entrance to the house.

The north front of the house is as Thomas Tropenell left it in 1480. It has well proportioned gables and two oriel windows with carved griffins holding the Tropenell Coat of Arms on the smaller and stone armoured knights at the points of the larger gables. The entrance porch which is at the centre has a stone groined ceiling with carved bosses as well as two figures at the western corners holding the Tropenell Coat of Arms. On entering the house there is a feeling that it must have been very snug inside, there are no winding passages through which the wind could howl, but a compact small plan with warmth rising from each succeeding floor. It is still possible to marvel at the strength and symmetry which Tropenell gave to his interiors way back in the 15th century, and when 200 years later Chalfield was garrisoned by Cromwell's troops, Tropenell's walls survived a short siege by Royalist troops under Goring.

Across the forecourt is Great Chalfield Parish Church of All Saints which possesses a notable series of wall paintings dating from the end of the 15th century. Thomas Tropenell seems to have refashioned the church, adding a chantry chapel on the south side of the nave, from which it is separated by a stone screen emblazoned with heraldry. The entire wall surface of the chapel was covered with paintings of which a considerable amount remains. Above the arch connecting with the nave is a shield with the Tropenell arms – gules, a fess engrailed ermine between three griffins' heads rased argent – with griffin supporters.

The paintings, though sadly mutilated, are clearly the work of a master who had a fine sense of colour and was, moreover, a skilled craftsman. These paintings managed to survive remarkably well until the middle of the 18th century, when through the efforts of some mindless people, the paintings were covered with a coat of limewash. It is only in recent years that the paintings were again exposed, but by now were very much in need of careful treatment.

In front of the north window stands a fine "three decker" pulpit, combining reader's desk, clerk's desk, and pulpit, a gift to the church by John Hall the 17th century owner of Chalfield. An attractive feature of the Nave, is the brass chandelier which hangs from the central beam and was given to the church by Major Fuller in 1914. It carries sixteen candles and is of the 17th century Flemish design.

In the Vestry which is parted from the Chancel by an oak screen, apparently brought from Kent in 1912, stands the beautiful little organ built by the Reverend Edward Kingston, who was rector here from 1878 to 1900. The casing which was added in 1914 was painted in the medieval manner by a Miss Maurice at the same time, and shows the "Three Wise Men" presenting their gifts to the Infant Jesus, one gift in the form of Chalfield Church.

The Hall or Kingston House
Bradford-on-Avon

Bradford-on-Avon was for centuries the centre of the West of England woollen-cloth manufacture, which reached its peak by the end of the 18th century. The town grew up at the "broad" ford crossing of the River Avon, long since given way to the 14th century bridge which became part of the historic route for pilgrims from Glastonbury to Malmesbury, and later to become the highway for the medieval trade in wool on its way from the West Country to southern ports shipping it to Flanders. By the middle of the 19th century the local cloth industry had lost out to the burgeoning competition of the Yorkshire mills, and Bradford-on-Avon was only saved from ruin by Stephen Moulton, who in 1848, purchased the Kingston Mill — formerly a cloth mill — upstream of the town bridge and started to make rubber. The organisation which he created is now part of the Avon Rubber Company.

The town is full of fine houses which belonged to the rich woolmasters during the heyday of the woollen industry, and to wander along its quaint streets is to walk into history. There are so many purlieus to explore and intimate little haunts to discover, where antique shops seem to nudge each other and to carry the detritus of centuries bought at today's prices.

Exploration will eventually bring you to "The Hall" situated on the right-hand side of Woolley Street leading to the Melksham road. This is the present home of the Moulton family, and the gardens are sometimes open to the public, but it is always advisable to enquire at the lodge at the entrance gates regarding admission. "The Hall" or Kingston House as it was originally called was built at the beginning of the 17th century for John Hall, a wealthy clothier, and it is a fine specimen of a classical house of the English renaissance. It displays an abundance of windows, and classical details, the character of which would suggest that the work could be of the same hand as Longleat. One writer said of the house in 1670 that "it is the best built house for the quality of a gentleman in Wiltshire".

The Hall, Bradford on Avon

The front of the house, which stands on a raised terrace, appears to be unusually tall for its depth, but it does display a highly decorative arrangement of bays and recesses, gables and battlements, characteristic of houses of that period which keeps it in balance.

After the extinction of the male line of the Hall family, Kingston House became through the last heiress, the property of the Dukes of Kingston, when it was known then as the "Duke's House". The house at one time was occupied by the notorious Elizabeth Chudleigh, who was known at various times as Mrs. Hervey, the Countess of Bristol, and finally as the Duchess of Kingston. Elizabeth was the daughter of Colonel and Mrs. Chudleigh of Chelsea, and was well connected with William Pulteney, Earl of Bath, who was at this time a Whig supporter in the House of Commons, and a great favourite with Frederick, Prince of Wales. Through this connection the tempestuous Elizabeth was introduced to the Court, and became at the age of eighteen a maid of honour to the Princess. A host of admirers sprang up around her, impressed with her beauty and her wit. One such young man was the Duke of Hamilton who proposed and was accepted by the ambitious young lady. Unfortunately it was discovered she had been having an affair with a certain Captain Augustus Hervey, and so to avoid a scandal, and the loss of her position at Court, Hervey and Elizabeth married discreetly, keeping the marriage secret. The raffish Hervey had few qualities to support the union, and within a short while the pair parted. Elizabeth left England for the continent where she appeared to enjoy the erotic frolics associated with the foreign courts she was attracted to. However her marriage with Hervey was a continuous source of irritation, and she even went as far as to visit the church where the marriage had first been celebrated and destroyed all records of the event. Nemesis was soon to dog her footsteps, she had now heard that Hervey had become the Earl of Bristol on the death of his father, but was himself in a declining state of health. As the new Duchess of Bristol, and hoping soon to be a wealthy dowager, she immediately took steps to restore the parish entry, only to find her husband had remarkably regained his health and strength. In a fit of pique she married Evelyn Pierrepont, Duke of Kingston, 1769. He was a man very much in his dotage and whose death could be expected in the near future.

Elizabeth had gained the height of her ambition as Duchess of Kingston, and the Duke of Bristol gave the lady an opportunity to obtain a divorce. The wily old Duke of Kingston very soon joined his ancestors, and although he had bequeathed his entire fortune to the Duchess, it was upon condition she should never marry again, and so the merry widow plunged into a life of one sordid intrigue after another. She was ridiculed by the actor Samuel Foote in a play "A Trip to Calais" where she is referred to as Lady Kitty Crocodile. There was an incident in Bath where she was involved in a dispute over payment to two Sedan chairmen, she refused payment and in the brouhaha that followed she presented the men with a piece of silver, worth many times the value of the chairmen's hire.

On the death of the Duchess the estate passed to the Duke's nephew, the son of his sister, Charles Meadows, who assumed the name and arms of Pierrepont, and was later created Earl Manvers in 1806.

"The Hall" and its surrounding garden under the care of the Moultons still remains a beautiful house and a joy to see, one must be impressed by the obvious desire of the owners to preserve their home, not just for themselves to live in, but for the many who visit the gardens during the summer months.

Hinton Priory
Near Freshford and Hinton Charterhouse

All the religious Orders, though differing in customs and in dress, were founded upon the general principle of a life in which the daily services of the church were the prime duty of the monastic establishment under the rule of an abbot or prior. Accordingly all monasteries may be said to have followed one general plan as regards the arrangement of the buildings necessary for the common life, with one exception, the houses of the Carthusian Order. The Order which was one of the strictest came to England in the 12th century, each monk had his separate cell, a small building with an upper room and with a plot of ground attached which he cultivated, but even here the cells were built round a cloister adjoining a church. There were but nine Carthusian monasteries or Charterhouses in England, and Hinton was the second foundation, whilst Witham near Frome in Somerset was the first.

Monks from Grande Chartreuse near Grenoble, came to Hinton and were settled by Ela the widow of the Earl of Salisbury in 1227. Building at Hinton was completed by 1232, and inaugurated by Ela on the same day, thought to be April 13th, as her nunnery at Lacock, and dedicated to the Virgin, St. John the Baptist, and All Saints.

Of Hinton there remains one beautiful 13th century building which was attached to the church on its south side. The church disappeared long ago, but the remainder is seen in three stages, the lowest is a fine vaulted chapel in three bays, showing on the south side a very remarkable spiral corbal, three lancet windows occupy the east wall, and on the north wall an ambry or cupboard. The first floor has another vaulted chamber in two bays, this is called the library, although there is nothing to suggest that it was ever used as such. The top floor is a dovecot with many nesting places.

Passing to the present stable-yard where further remains of the priory can still be located. Standing east to west and still showing its two storeys is the frater. Under the Carthusian rule the brethren did not meet in the frater or refectory everyday, but only on Sundays and feast-

16th Century House, Hinton Priory

days. On other days they kept within their little house, which was occupied by one monk, each with his own garden. The best example of a Charterhouse extant today, and showing these old arrangements, is Mount Grace Priory, a Carthusian house in Yorkshire not far from Osmotherley. Founded in 1398, it was the last monastery to be built in the County.

At the time of the Dissolution it was estimated that there were about 650 monasteries in England and that between them they owned a quarter of the land. The first blow at the existing order of things was dealt from within the Church. Cardinal Wolsey obtained leave from the Pope to dissolve a number of small houses and devote their revenues to the endowment of two great colleges which he was to promote at Oxford and Ipswich. It is more than likely this step gave Henry the idea of more sweeping measures. In 1535 to 1536 a Bill was passed for the suppression of all houses under the clear annual value of £200, and in 1539 another Act was passed investing the property of all surviving houses in the king. Henry cut England off from Rome and proclaimed himself head of the Church, and brought the clergy and their monies into subservience to the Crown. This seizing of monastic property meant the biggest change in land ownership since the Conquest. Much of the Church property was given away to Henry's courtiers and hangers-on.

Thomas Cromwell's "investigators" reached Hinton in March 1540. They arrived without ceremony, demanded to see Prior Hood

41

who surrendered the monastery to Henry VIII on the 31st of the month. There was nowhere for these unfortunate monks to go, because there were no longer any religious houses left for them to join, and so they were given a small pension or the alternative to serve Henry's new breakaway church.

It was left to Matthew Colthurst the man who allowed decay to settle on Bath Abbey, to purchase Hinton allowing the same to happen to this once proud house. The wealthy Hungerfords of nearby Farleigh, who already owned most of the land in the neighbourhood, purchased the site from Colthurst, and immediately set about dismantling the buildings, the stones of which were used later in the building of the nearby Tudor mansion. The gatehouse of the Priory was converted and forms one of the major wings of the reconstructed building. The south and west elevations are gabled with stone mullioned windows of Elizabethan design, whilst the north front still bear traces of the original monastery buildings. The interior has some excellent panelling and two interesting staircases.

Sir Edward Hungerford sold the Priory to the Robinsons, passing eventually to Major P. C. Fletcher who carried out a considerable amount of excavations, in fact much of what is seen today of the monastic buildings is attributed to his considerable enthusiasm. The present owner is Mr. Jack Raeburn.

History has inclined to treat monasteries with undeserved odium, they were not the hotbeds of crime and luxury, many were somnolent, many may have been insolvent, few were evil.

Hinton Priory

Horton Court
Near Chipping Sodbury, Avon

A Cotswold manor house thought to be the oldest inhabited house in England. This is the claim made by the National Trust the present owners, for Horton Court a beautiful building just three miles NE of the old cloth and cheese town of Chipping Sodbury. It stands close beside the ancient church of Horton, and is certainly one of the most interesting and historic private residences in the West of England. Building commenced about 1100 and during this period onwards the north wing was completed. The Tudor additions followed later and though different in style, the two periods blend perfectly.

Posterity's debt for the Norman wing is to Robert de Bella-Fago, a great Oxford scholar, and a prebendary of Salisbury Cathedral. The high hall, with its Norman windows, and its two doorways, the strongly defined zig-zag mouldings of which are almost as perfect as when they left the Norman mason's hands. The ancient hall was once divided into two storeys, but happily it has been restored to its original plan showing the space open to the roof. The Norman house earned a reputation for the brewing and drinking of ale, and apparently de Bella-Fago being something of a poet wrote a series of poems "In Praise of Ale".

During the 14th century the manor of Horton passed into the Knight family. One member a William Knight became a Doctor of Law, and a secretary to Henry VIII. He took a prominent part in the negotiations for the divorce of Henry and Catherine of Aragon. It was William Knight who extended the Manor, fortunately retaining the Norman wing. For a short period he was sent to Rome and returned impressed with the new building styles of the Eternal City, and so burgeoning with ideas on how to build in the Renaissance style as he had known it in Italy he set about making alterations at Horton. In the garden he built an ambulatory, which today remains wonderfully well preserved. Its arcade of arches faces the trim, sloping lawn, and on the stone wall at the rear are four large medallions in plaster of the Caesars which he brought back from Rome.

44

Horton Court

In 1708 the house belonged to the Pastons, and it was during their ownership that the flooring dividing the Norman hall into two storeys was put in. The Pastons had remained Catholics, and this upper storey was used as a chapel, and a priest was installed and maintained there. Indeed there is still a secret passage leading from the house to the part which once served for a chapel.

The property came into the possession of the National Trust in 1949 under the will of Miss Hilda Wills, in memory of her nephew, Sir Peter Wills, Bt. killed in action in 1945 during the Second World War.

Whichever way you approach Horton Court the route to follow is along narrow lanes with here and there passing places, but this Cotswold country, and the views towards the Severn and beyond into Wales are incomparable, and the manor, ensconced in such delightful surroundings away from the beaten track makes a visit well worth while.

Lansdown Crescent, and Lansdown Place West, including Beckford's Tower, Bath

Charles Spackman, coach builder turned property speculator, was the genius behind the building of Lansdown Crescent. The architect John Palmer was employed to design the layout for this terrace of houses, and work was commenced about 1789. Palmer's difficulties were the curving slopes of Lansdown, and the serpentine scheme which finally emerged is a tribute to his professionalism.

On completion the crescent came to be known as Spackman's Buildings, later as The Upper Crescent, and finally as Lansdown Crescent. Number 20 is the terminal house of the centre segment, and in 1822 it became the Bath residence of the author and eccentric William Beckford. To understand this extraordinary man we must go back a few years prior to the restoration of Charles II. The Beckfords were considered of importance and occupied a strong position among those speculating their wealth in the West Indies. Colonel Peter Beckford settled for the newly acquired island of Jamaica, and his private fortune kept pace with the burgeoning development which took place once the island was secured under British rule. He died in 1710 possessed of a considerable fortune, and having served William III as Commander-in-Chief of the forces in Jamaica. His eldest son Peter Beckford was Speaker of the House of Assembly who increased his wealth further by a rich marriage. However Peter's son William returned to England and became Lord Mayor of London, he loved the rich and peachy environment of London society. He never returned to Jamaica, but he eventually purchased Fonthill in Wiltshire where he built a grand Palladian mansion and called it "Splendens", and here he brought his wife Maria, daughter and co-heiress of George Hamilton M.P. They had one son William who was only ten years old when his father died in 1770, and at this tender age he found himself possessed of his father's immense fortune, and the estates at Fonthill-Gifford.

In 1782 he married Lady Margaret Gordon, daughter of the Earl of Aboyne, and shortly afterwards became M.P. for Wells in Somerset. But literature and the arts made greater claims upon him

William Beckford's House, Lansdown Crescent

and he soon found that politics bored him. He wrote "Vathek" in French at a single sitting of three days and two nights, and so finally discarding the Parliamentary life, left England for Portugal to lead a life of a dilettante. Byron described him as "England's wealthiest son".

On returning to this country his eccentric genius conceived the idea for building Fonthill Abbey. It was to be a magnificent building of remarkable dimensions, built in the form of a cross with a central tower rising to the great height of 278 feet. In 1807 this mammoth building was occupied, 15 years later it was sold, Beckford was in dire financial difficulties, it was impossible for him to continue to live like some oriental panjandrum, and so he came to Bath, and purchased 20 Lansdown Crescent. Shortly afterwards the gigantic tower at Fonthill collapsed, the foundations were found to be totally inadequate for this type of construction, but the architect James Wyatt was beyond the reach of censure for he had died earlier in a coaching accident.

Beckford's lifestyle altered little, he continued to live his life amiable and aloof, but now possessed more than ever by his love of books and animals. His passion for privacy compelled him to purchase the terminal house of Lansdown Place West, joining it to No. 20 Lansdown Crescent by a bridge. He made reluctant headlines at the time, and the following appeared in the Bath Chronicle. "Mr. Beckford is arrived at his house in Lansdown Crescent and engaged in making extensive alterations and arrangements for his unique pictures, books, and

Lansdown Crescent

Beckford's Tower

other rare and costly specimens of art. It is reported that this Gentleman is in treaty for an extensive portion of land in the rear of the Crescent, with a view of erecting a building on the same. We sincerely hope this is no idle rumour; the site is admirably calculated for the exercise of Mr. Beckford's classic taste and we may anticipate a model of architectural beauty not unworthy of Rome in the climax of its splendour; and which may also serve as a memorial of Mr. Beckford's munificence, and prove a real ornament to the city to which it pertains."

The public were expecting too much, an unbroken stretch of land at the rear of his two houses was certainly purchased and transformed into a series of elaborate plantations, partly wilderness and partly gardens. Beckford who loved a prospect found that Lansdown Crescent afforded an incomplete viewpoint and so he decided to build his second tower, selecting the highest point of his garden on which to construct his whimsy. The building was designed by Henry Goodridge and was completed by 1827.

Tower Stairs, Beckford Tower after restoration

Surmounting the new tower was a model of the Choragic Monument of Lysicrates at Athens, under this was a square room, on each side of which were three arched windows. In the entrance hall was a table of Sienna marble, on which were Etruscan vases. Everywhere were paintings and sculptures, a real treasure trove, and in addition to all this was Beckford's magnificent library. It has been said that necessity forced him to sell his pictures, but he never, till his death, parted with a book.

In 1829 Beckford was involved in a dispute with Bath Corporation over rights of way across his land. He wrote to the mayor threatening to leave Bath, and to allow his land to be used to build a town "of not less than 1500 hovels". This threat did not go unheeded, and he was allowed to close a certain number of footpaths. In return he built a gravel walk with trees on either side for use by the public.

Beckford's reluctance to mix socially and his non-conformity started a whispering campaign of character assassination. He was supposed to have kept a retinue of dwarfs with the implied sinister overtones, when in fact he had only one dwarf, his constant companion Perro, whom he had befriended whilst travelling abroad and brought back to England, where he continued to act as Beckford's servant and friend.

Beckford died at Bath in May 1844 aged 84, and his one wish was to be buried near a favourite dog, and in the shade of his tower. Unfortunately this was denied him, the ground being unconsecrated, and so his burial took place in the Abbey cemetery. However Beckford's daughter, the Duchess of Hamilton, some time afterwards managed to obtain possession of the tower site, apparently it was sold at auction in 1847 with the intention of being turned into a tavern. The Duchess prevented this indignity by re-purchasing it, and presenting it to the parish of Walcot. The land and tower was now consecrated to become a chapel and cemetery for the parish. Beckford had his wish, his remains were exhumed and returned to the spot he loved so well.

In recent years the parish of Walcot have tried to rid themselves of this "pain in the neck", a reference paid to it by the rector, but Doctor Leslie Hilliard and his wife Elizabeth of Batheaston had more worthwhile ideas. They considered the tower to be a local amenity, offering access to its summit so that people could enjoy the superb views of Bath and the surrounding countryside. The tower was purchased by them, and with a Government grant, they completely restored the building, and during the summer the public now have access. Dr. and Mrs. Hilliard have now transferred the tower with an endowment to the newly created Beckford Tower Trust, thus securing the tower's future.

It is still possible to obtain some idea of Beckford's retreat, and by wandering to the rear of his houses in Lansdown Crescent there are traces of his kitchen gardens, and the walls which still retain an embattled gateway leading to the now vanished route to his tower.

Lacock Abbey
Lacock, Wilts.

Time has dealt kindly with the Wiltshire village of Lacock. Its old stone houses and half-timbered buildings seem untouched with the passage of years, and where modern buildings have been erected they conform to the general character of the existing dwellings.

The village of Lacock grew up round the wool trade, and many of the rooms in the cottages had to be wide enough to accommodate the broadloom that wove cloth a hundred inches wide. The village was so important as a centre of the West of England woollen industry during the 17th and 18th centuries that the London to Bath coaches risked the descent of Bowden Hill in order to stop there, depositing the wealthy woolmasters at the welcoming sign of the Red Lion Inn where the sole topic of conversation would be the current prices of wool. The inn was given a handsome brick facade in Georgian times.

The greater part of the village had always belonged to the owners of the 13th century Abbey which was converted into a private residence in 1540. Ela, the daughter and heiress of the Earl of Salisbury founded the nunnery here in 1232, and successive owners have loved and preserved the property until in 1944 it was presented to the National Trust by the last private owner, Miss Matilda Talbot.

Ela took the habit of Lacock in 1238, which was then under the rule of St. Augustine, and in 1240 became its Abbess. The history of the Abbey from then on seems to have been uneventful until the suppression, when the monastic buildings and the village was granted to Sir William Sharington on June 16th 1540 at a cost of £783 on condition that the nuns were awarded pensions for their lifetime.

Sharington in many ways was something of a rogue. He was obviously a very wealthy man, and at one time a member of the Royal Household of Henry VIII. At Edward VI's Coronation he was knighted and made Vice-Treasurer of the Bristol Mint. He was always quick to sense a rotten plank and to move before it broke, and he himself was spared, which contributed to his success in all his undertakings, but life was uncertain in those days and already Sharington

51

Lacock Abbey

was deeply involved in intrigue with Lord Seymour against Protector Somerset. The final act came when he was found out debasing the coinage and falsifying the accounts of the Mint. He was arrested in 1549, together with Seymour who was charged with more serious crimes against the state. Seymour's estates became forfeit by Act of Parliament, and he was eventually executed. Whereas Sharington, having placed the blame fully and squarely on Seymour lost his lands but saved his head. Later he was pardoned, and on payment of £8000 regained all his estates which included his prize possession the village of Lacock. The document granting his pardon is still preserved at Lacock.

Whatever doubts one may hold regarding Sharington's many shortcomings, he certainly had a keen eye for architecture, and the preservation of the many monastic buildings of the Abbey, which included the sacristy, the chapter house, and cloisters which were largely his responsibility. Furthermore he converted the Abbey into a fine mansion by adding a Tudor courtyard and other domestic buildings, which display his skills derived from the period he spent in Italy and the influence of the Renaissance builders. Unfortunately the great church of Ela which occupied the southern side of the cloisters was destroyed during these alterations.

Although Sharington had married three times he had no children, and so on his death he was succeeded by his brother Henry, whose daughter Olive married John Talbot of Salwarpe near Worcester, and so the Talbots came to Lacock. Olive survived both her husband and her son who had taken the name of Sharington Talbot, and so on her death the estates passed to her grandson in 1646.

During the Civil War Lacock was occupied at different times by both Parliamentary and King's forces. Sharington Talbot's sympathies

Cloisters, Lacock Abbey

were with the King and for this he was fined £1100 after the war had finished. The continuing support for the Stuarts at the Restoration paid off, and Sharington Talbot's son John was given the accolade of knighthood, and further honours were to come for in 1663 Charles II visited Lacock as the guest of Sir John.

On the death of Sir John Talbot in 1714 the estates passed to his grandson John Ivory, the son of his daughter Anne and her husband Sir John Ivory. The young John Ivory added Talbot to his name and proved to be a capable administrator of his property, and finished up with a seat in Parliament as the member for Wiltshire. He set about making considerable changes at Lacock, sweeping away those fussy, geometrically planned formal gardens which was the fashion of the 17th century, and redesigned the landscape in order to create a vista of the countryside beyond, from the house.

In 1753 he met the architect Sanderson Miller, at a period when there arose a tendency in style of "looking back" to bygone times. The new "Gothick" was popularised by Horace Walpole, and Miller appeared as an architect with kindred tastes. So Miller was commissioned to rebuild the Great Hall in this style, adding its flight of steps, and the archway to the carriage drive.

Ivory Talbot died in 1772, and his son having died childless, the estates passed to his daughter Martha, wife of the Reverend William Davenport. Their son William added Talbot to his name and married the brilliant Lady Elizabeth Fox-Strangeways, daughter of the Earl of Ilchester. They had a son William Henry Fox Talbot, born in 1800, and like his mother a brilliant scholar. He went to Harrow in 1811, where he made exceptional progress, and later he went up to Trinity College, Cambridge, where he obtained First Class Honours in Classics. In 1832 he married a Constance Munby and it was during their honeymoon in Europe he started to develop his ideas of making his own image by photographic reproduction.

Returning to Lacock, Fox Talbot began his dramatic sequence of discoveries. In 1833 he began the research and experiments which culminated in the invention of photography, an invention which has been called the greatest since printing.

Now the National Trust has made available the 16th century barn at the gates of the Abbey for a museum to commemorate the invention of photography by Fox Talbot, and which now contains an exhibition illustrating the life and work of this most distinguished scholar.

Charles Henry Talbot, William's son, owned the property from 1877 to 1916, when it was bequeathed to his niece Matilda Theresa, the daughter of his sister Matilda Caroline. On succeeding to the estates Matilda Theresa adopted the name of Talbot, and in 1944 she presented the Abbey with the village to the National Trust.

Linley House
1 Pierrepont Place and Orchard Street, Bath

St. James' portico was built by John Wood about 1730, and is described by him as being "No more than a way left in the basement storey of the first row of houses extending from the Grand Parade to the Royal Forum for a communication with horses and carriages between the body of the city and the new building at the south east corner of it". The Grand Parade referred to by Wood is of course North Parade, and the site of the proposed "Royal Forum" is now occupid by St. John's Catholic Church and the adjoining car park. Pierrepont Street, named after the Pierrepont family, was built in 1727 to link the two sites. John Wood went on to add, "and for its length is the most beautiful street in the City". Mark you, at that time, Bath as a Georgian city was still in the embryo stage.

St. James' Portico was built to give access to Orchard Street without breaking the uniformity of the street elevation, the portico forming the ground floor of the house, and the upper part being carried on four Doric columns surmounted by a modillioned pediment.

Orchard Street takes its name from the fact that it is built on the site of the ancient Abbey orchard. At the far end where it joins Henry Street is a building which in turn has served the purposes of a theatre, a Roman Catholic Chapel, and is now used as a Masonic Hall. Bath was sadly lacking in theatrical accommodation until 1747 when a John Hippisley, a London actor of considerable ability, planned the Orchard Street Theatre. Unfortunately he died before the building was completed, but John Palmer a prosperous brewer who had married into the distinguished Wiltshire family of the Longs promoted the theatre further and the doors were opened for the first performance in 1750. However it was Palmer's son, John Palmer the Younger who at the age of 26, when the theatre was facing a crises, successfully petitioned Parliament for a grant of letters patent enabling the theatre to use the title, "Theatre Royal", the first to be given this distinction outside London. It is true to say that John

Linley House

Palmer is best remembered for his pioneering of the first English mailcoach. He met considerable opposition at first from the Post Office, but with some assistance from William Pitt, then Chancellor of the Exchequer, the service commenced with the first mailcoach leaving Bristol on August 2 1784, calling at the Three Tuns Inn in Bath, and on to London. In 1786 Palmer was appointed Surveyor and Comptroller General of the Mails, but the gerontocracy working within the Post Office was critical of his schemes for improving the mail service. By 1792 matters had reached a climax, and he was forced to leave the Post Office altogether.

The Portico end of Orchard Street is now known as Pierrepont Place, and at No. 1 lived the Linley family. The house which is also known as Linley House after this talented family, was designed by John Wood in 1742 for a plasterer named John Hutchins. In the middle 1960's a consortium which included Mrs. Barbara Robertson of Combe Hay and the Bath architect Hugh Roberts purchased the house. This fine house was now in sympathetic hands, and work was commenced to restore the building to its pristine state. The entrance doorway remains quite unaltered, retaining its Ionic pilasters supporting two pineapples on a projecting straight hood. The interior displays much of its original decoration, and is among the best of its period surviving in Bath. The Music Room shows the plasterer's craft to advantage in the enrichment of the ceiling, which features a fine modillioned cornice with scallop shells, pine-apples, and baskets of fruit and flowers enclosed in L-shaped corner panels.

The musical Linley family lived in the house from 1767–1771, having formerly lived at No. 6 Pierrepont Street. In this house during the month of September 1754, the "Fair Maid of Bath", Elizabeth Linley was born. At sixteen she was already a beautiful and talented young lady, and sang with some distinction at her father's concerts. Gainsborough who was then living in the Circus painted her portrait several times, and one hangs in the National Gallery in Washington, and another of Elizabeth and her sister Mary, later known as "Betty Tickle" on marrying Richard Tickle, can be seen at the Dulwich Gallery.

It was after the family had moved to the Royal Crescent, that the love affair between Elizabeth, now 18, and Richard Sheridan crystallised into their elopement and marriage in France. On returning to England Sheridan was involved in a duel with a Captain Mathews, a former admirer of Elizabeth, however the Captain came off worse, and his final humiliation was an apology in the Bath Chronicle of the day.

The Linely family left Bath in 1775 and went to London where Thomas Linley had now been appointed musical director of Drury Lane Theatre. His son Tom, composer and violinist, and friend of Mozart enjoyed little of the success he was destined to have, for at the age of 22, three years after coming to London he died. Mention must be made here of one other member of this household who lived at Linley House, and who later achieved notoriety and fame. This was Emma Hart, the Linley's servant girl who later married Sir William Hamilton, and became the mistress of Lord Nelson.

Linley House is now the headquarters of the Bath Festival Society.

Little Sodbury Manor
Near Chipping Sodbury, Avon

Little Sodbury Manor lies just off the A432 Chipping Sodbury road, and north of the village of Old Sodbury. It takes its name from the neighbouring Roman fort on the summit of the hill close by and which was created with many others to command the course of the River Severn and to give protection from the incursions of the hostile tribes from the West. The manor house is beautifully situated on the south western escarpment of the Cotswold Hills, and enjoys magnificent views over the richly-wooded vale of the Severn, and beyond to the distant hills of Wales.

After the Conquest the manor was held by the Bishop of Lisieux until the time of Edward II, an unfortunate monarch, who persisted in surrounding himself with unpopular favourites, in particular Hugh le Despenser and his son. The Despensers came to live at the manor until their final disgrace and the execution of the elder at Bristol, and the younger at Hereford on gallows fifty feet high.

By the beginning of the 15th century the Stanshaw family were living at the manor, and it was this family who in 1450 built the earliest portions of the present house including the hall. The Stanshaws were followed by Richard Foster and it was his daughter on marrying John Walsh of Olveston who set about improving the property. Their son who became Sir John Walsh did much to improve the house and the estate, and he was more than fortunate in marrying Anne the daughter of Sir Robert Poyntz, of Iron Acton. But his greatest claim to fame was his association with William Tyndale, reformer and translator of the Bible. Tyndale came into the Walsh family as chaplain and tutor to Sir John's children. The Walshes of Little Sodbury were one of the rising and prosperous families of the country, and Sir John, the patron and employer of Tyndale had been champion to Henry VIII on more than one occasion, and having been fortunate enough to secure the support of his king, he was knighted and given the more substantial adjoining manor of Old Sodbury, which had devolved to the crown from the Countess of Warwick.

Little Sodbury Manor

History recalls that in the great dining-hall Tyndale was so often heard debating theological points with the local clergy around the hospitable table of Sir John. At this time Tyndale was planning his translation of the Bible for which he is justly famous. It was while serving his patron at Little Sodbury that he made his decision to undertake this colossal task so that he could bring its teaching to the common people. Matters were getting out of hand so in 1523 he left the Walsh family, and with the goodwill of his patron he departed for London, where he eventually sailed for Hamburg in 1524. It was the printer Schoeffer who published the translation, but copies arriving in England were confiscated and burned. In 1535 he was staying in Antwerp with Thomas Poyntz, a relative of Lady Walsh of Sodbury. At this house he was arrested, charged with heresy, and finally burnt at the stake.

Just north of Wotton-under-Edge is a monument perched on an outcrop of the Cotswolds, it is known as Nibley Knoll and overlooks the village of North Nibley where Tyndale was born and spent much of his early life. The monument on the Knoll was erected to commemorate his association with the village and his work and final sacrifice.

There is a sad story to relate concerning the Walsh family. The year was 1556 and Sir John's son Maurice and his family were dining when the manor was struck by lightning killing all the members of the family sitting down to dinner. The Walsh line did not come to an end as a result of this calamity, but continued to live at Little Sodbury until 1608, when the manor and the lands were purchased by Thomas

59

Stephens. It was his son Henry who made the 17th century additions to the house.

In 1728 Robert Packer of Donington Castle became the owner and through marriage the manor passed into the Hartley family. By the end of the 19th century general neglect was next to assail the house and gardens, and it was in a poor state by the time the ninth Duke of Beaufort bought Little Sodbury from the Hartleys and made some attempt at restoration. It was however Baron de Tuyll, step-son of the Duke of Beaufort who purchased in 1919, who really started to refurbish and restore the property, in fact the eastern end of the north wing had fallen down by that time and the architect Sir Harold Brakspear was commissioned to design a completely new wing to include a new dining-room area. The Baron lived there until he died, when after a short interval the estate was sold to Mr. Mark Harford a descendant of John Scandrett Harford who built Blaise Castle House and Blaise Hamlet more than one hundred and fifty years earlier.

The present owner is Gerald Harford who will allow visitors to see his beautiful Cotswold manor house providing arrangements are made beforehand.

The Manor House Mells, Somerset

The Manor House which abuts the 15th century church of St. Andrews at Mells is now the home of the Earl of Oxford. The house dates from 1590 when it was built by one John Horner, a local landowner. Horner engaged a local master mason to build for him with instructions that the mansion should be built in the shape of the letter H, unfortunately in recent years the house has been altered and two wings have been demolished.

The story of Mells goes far back to pre-Reformation times, when the village and manor formed part of the great holding of the Somerset estates of Glastonbury Abbey. It was Abbot Thomas Selwood, a native of Frome, who in 1490 worked out a grand plan to rebuild Mells in the manner of a Roman City, and although a start was made little was completed, now all that remains of this grandiose scheme is the High Street, which runs quite straight without any irregularity through the village, and New Street which leads to the church, and where many of the doorways still have the monogram of Thomas Selwood – T.S. – over them, and over the doorway of the Horner sister's house Thomas Selwood's coat of arms may be seen.

Nevertheless Mells prospered and thrived upon a flourishing woollen industry, and along the pastures of Vallis Vale, beside the River Frome and the Mells stream grazed black cattle, and stocky sheep that brought wealth to the woolmasters and hardwork to the many, and as if to expiate themselves for their wealth, these merchants poured their excess cash into the building and adorning the fine perpendicular churches of Somerset.

Every child will know of it, and every grown-up was nurtured on it, for it is the story of Little Jack Horner and his plum. The old nursery rhyme based on the satirical writing of a 16th century wit refers to a John Horner of Cloford who was Glastonbury's bailiff at Mells. In 1535 Thomas Cromwell called for the surrender of the deeds of the Manor of Mells, together with twelve others belonging to the Glaston-

The Manor House, Mells

bury Abbey. They were hidden in a pie and entrusted to John Horner to deliver to Cromwell, but on the way curiosity compelled him to lift the crust and his cupidity being what it was he removed the deeds to the Manor of Mells and kept them for himself. One of the great imponderables of history, of course, had it been true Jack Horner would certainly have pulled out a plum, but the truth of the matter the property was legally purchased from Henry's Commissioners by Thomas Horner, and his descendants have lived at Mells to this day. In many ways it was indeed a plum, for the countryside around Mells has a lush and rounded aspect, gentle, undramatic, but peaceful.

The Horners became involved in local politics, and were staunch supporters of the Liberal cause, so much so that Katherine, daughter of Sir John Horner, married Raymond Asquith son of the Liberal Prime Minister, Herbert Henry Asquith to become later 1st Earl of Oxford and Asquith, and who died in 1928. World War I treated both the Horners and the Asquiths harshly. Sir John's heir and last of the male line, Edward Horner, and Raymond Asquith were both killed in action in 1917, and when Sir John died in 1927 the manor and estates passed to Mrs. Raymond Asquith.

This is the land of splendid medieval towers, and regal and richly decorated churches. The great church at Mells is no exception, built of the local stone, it has many interesting features to show. The altar cloth was worked by Lady Frances Horner, and a fine tapestry, another tribute by this lady, portrays a guardian angel taken from a design by Burne-Jones, friend of William Morris, socialist and a pre-

Raphaelite. There is a particularly interesting memorial to Edward Horner who was killed at Cambrai in 1917. It is an imposing equestrian statue in bronze sculptured by Sir Alfred Munnings, and set on a pedestal by Sir Edwin Lutyens, a touching tribute by the Horner family to a noble son.

Among the headstones in the churchyard is one dedicated to Ronald Arbuthnot Knox who died in 1957. He was priest and scholar, and after some years as a fellow and chaplain of Trinity College, Oxford, he joined the Roman Catholic Church in 1917, and so he came to Mells and became a frequent guest at the Manor House where he completed his famous translation of the Bible. Mrs. Raymond Asquith's conversion to the Catholic faith created at Mells a small enclave of converts. Another headstone bearing the stamp of Lutyens supports the name of Reginald McKenna, Liberal politician and one time Chairman of the Midland Bank, and his wife Pamela. They lived for many years at nearby Mells Park House which had been built by the Horners in 1740, but altered and mostly rebuilt by Lutyens for the McKennas in 1923. During the occupancy of the Park House by the Horners, Lady Horner created there a great meeting place for Liberal politicians, and many famous names celebrated for their nimble and witty conversation would gather there.

Mells Manor House is not open to the public, but a glimpse of its fine old gables can be seen from the churchyard, or from the stables next to the Talbot Inn where Lady Oxford has opened a garden shop. Pevsner succinctly describes the scene in his "Buildings of England" (North Somerset). "The group of church and manor-house is among the happiest in Somerset, the tower appearing strong and trustworthy above the high trimmed hedges of the garden."

Montacute House
Near Yeovil, Somerset

Under the brow of St. Michael's Hill, conspicuous with its lookout tower, lies the charming Ham stone village of Montacute, and nearby the grand Elizabethan mansion of Montacute House. The hill has passed into legend, for in the days of Canute his standard bearer Tofig held lands here and was also lord of Waltham in Essex. A smith in the village of Leodgaresburh – the Saxon name given to the village of Montacute – was persistently troubled by a vision in which he was told to dig on the top of St. Michael's Hill, and so, Tofig thinking in terms of gold ordered his servants to dig on the hilltop. Their industry was rewarded for after considerable effort the servants found a great stone which split open to disclose a crucifix of black flint. It was decided to take the crucifix to Canterbury, but the journey ended at Tofig's hunting lodge on the edge of Waltham Forest, Tofig was greatly impressed with his find, and on the site of his hunting lodge he built and founded the abbey of the "Holy Cross" as a safe repository for this remarkable treasure. Harold the last of the Saxon kings established here a house of secular canons, and the battle cry of "Holy Cross" was used by Harold's men at the battle of Hastings.

This story has nothing to do directly with Montacute House or Montacute Priory, but it made both places famous, and deserves to be mentioned. The Priory was Cluniac and was founded in 1102 by William, Count of Mortain in Normandy. He also built a feudal castle on "Mons acutus", the pointed hill, which later gave the name to Montacute village. Of the castle nothing remains, and all that is left of the once wealthy and splendid Priory is a fine 15th century gatehouse. Its stately archway is surmounted by a well preserved oriel window corbelled above the great door. Another oriel is located on the other side of the archway between two stair turrets, both oriels carrying the initials of Thomas Chard prior from 1514 to 1532.

Soon after the gatehouse was completed the Cluniacs left, and it would seem that about this time, the Priory and its lands were taken over by Thomas Phelips, already a successful landowner. Now this

The East Front, Montacute House

Thomas had a grandson also called Thomas, and it is with this member of the Phelips family that the story of Montacute House begins.

Thomas abandoned the monastic buildings in order to build his famous house, but it was left to the youngest son Edward to complete. Edward Phelips by 1587 was a successful lawyer at the Middle Temple, and as Master of the Rolls led the indictment against Guy Fawkes. In the reign of James I he became Speaker of the House of Commons, and in 1603 he received his knighthood. Work at Montacute probably began about 1588, and from the date over the east porch, the house was finished in 1601. The H-shaped designed mansion is surrounded by gardens and parklands, and is the work of the master mason, William Arnold. The eastern side is approached through a forecourt enclosed by an elaborate balustrade linking two stone pavilions at the corners to the mansion. Over the east doorway, originally the main entrance, are carved the date 1601, and the arms of the Phelips family. The facade is richly ornamented, shell-shaped niches between the mullioned windows being occupied by statues of the Nine Worthies dressed as Roman soldiers.

The West front, now the main entrance, approached from the road through wrought iron gates and by means of a drive that runs between billiard table lawns, was built in 1786. Sir Thomas Phelips bought the porch and other ornamental features of a Tudor house some distance away in Dorset, called Clifton Maybank, and fitted them quite boldly between the two wings of the West front. Although the Dorset facade comes from a house fifty years older than Mon-

65

tacute, it harmonizes well with Montacute's Renaissance detail, furthermore it was built from the same Ham stone that weathers with the years to a more golden tone.

Elegant as the exterior is, it gives little hint of the spaciousness and dignity that lies within. The Great Hall is 50 feet long by 21 feet wide, and possesses a finely sculptured stone screen, and the Great Chamber is nearly as big. Both have classical chimney pieces of stone, windows containing glass illustrating the history of the Phelips family, patterned ceilings and friezes of richly ornamental plasterwork displaying swags of flowers and fruit. Over the north door out of the Great Hall is an elaborate plaster frieze showing an ancient village ritual.

Upstairs is the Long Gallery measuring 180 feet into the oriel windows at each end, which provided in those early days a fine playground for generations of children, and a place where Elizabethan ladies would walk on wet days when walking in their elaborate gowns made it difficult in the gardens. Once more the gallery serves a useful purpose, for on display here and in the adjoining rooms is the National Portrait Gallery's collection of Elizabethan and Jacobean portraits which for many years had not seen the light of day until exhibited here. It meant too that cleaning, restoration, and reframing work had to be carried out, which in most cases had never been done before, and which revealed some startling transformations in the appearance of the pictures.

Only one family, the Phelips family, has owned Montacute House since Sir Edward Phelips built it. He died at Wanstead in 1614 and is

Garden Pavilion, Montacute House

buried at Montacute. Robert Phelips succeeded his father to the title and the estates, and later became involved in politics, a dangerous pastime at that time, by opposing Charles I in parliament. Robert's grandson Edward was succeeded by a nephew, whose son, the fifth Edward came into possession in 1734 at the age of nine, holding the property for over 60 years. With the death of the Rev. William Phelips, son of the fifth Edward, in 1806, his son John succeeded. He was best known for his philanthropy, and it is said that he would wander around the countryside giving work to the unemployed.

By the beginning of the First World War the Phelips family had ceased to live at Montacute, and from 1915 to 1925 the property was leased to Lord Curzon, who proved a most appreciative tenant, keeping the mansion in impeccable order. Eventually it was sold in 1931 when it was bought by the well known patron of the arts, collector, and public benefactor Ernest Cook of Bath, on behalf of the Society for the Protection of Ancient Buildings, and in due course it was handed over to the National Trust.

Owlpen Manor
Near Uley, Gloucestershire

Uley is a small town set on a peaceful sweep of the Cotswold Hills. It is a wool village of some antiquity, and its High Street is as pretty a place as you could hope to find anywhere with some of the best 17th and 18th century houses in the country. Most of the town is preserved as being of historical and architectural interest. Here lived John Eyles, and it was his weaving of the fine Spanish cloth that made Uley famous. That is not all which makes Uley important, for just north of the town is the important Stone Age barrow known as Hetty Pegler's Tump, and where the views from the top of the tumulus extend right

Owlpen Manor, Uley

across the Severn valley into the Welsh mountains. Also lying in a hollow of the hills below Uley is Owlpen Manor House, a Cotswold stone house of 15th century origin, with its splendid little church just above it and a water mill not far away.

The earlier building was the home of the Ollepen family in the 13th century, and was known then as Ollepen Manor. Later the name was changed to Oldpen, but in the 19th century the name was changed once more to Owlpen Old Manor, possibly because of the owls shown on the Ollepen coat of arms.

John Daunt came into the Owlpen property on his marriage to the heiress Marjorie Ollepen in 1464. Daunt set about refurbishing the property and the house owes its present style to successive generations of the Daunt family. It was Thomas Daunt, the grandson of John, who rebuilt the hall and the great chamber above on the site of the earlier house.

Another Thomas Daunt rebuilt the West wing, and the embattled bay window bears his initials and the date 1616. His son another Thomas married Catherine Clayton of Chester, and their grandson Thomas married Elizabeth Synge. Thomas and Elizabeth came to live at Owlpen in the early 18th century and carried out the last of the many alterations made to the manor house. Elizabeth died in 1757 and the property then came into the possession of Achilles Daunt the younger son. It was the granddaughter of Achilles who eventually inherited, and on marrying Thomas Anthony Stoughton of County Kerry the property came into that family.

The Stoughtons considered Owlpen too small for their occupation and so, in 1850 they built a far grandeur house on the hillside above the manor. This house was in the neo-classical style and had a series of extensive out buildings and splendid gardens. The house no longer exists, for in 1955 it was sold and later demolished.

The old manor meanwhile had remained unused, but was kept in a reasonable state of repair. In 1925 it was purchased by a Norman Jewson who carried out a skillfull restoration of the whole property. The Manor today is in ownership of Mrs. Bray who has shown considerable thought in furnishing and equipping the house in sympathy with the many styles and periods of its history. Its great attraction are the clipped yews, many of which were planted two hundred years ago.

Prior Park
Near Bath

Prior Park is Bath's most memorable man-made landmark, standing high on Combe Down where it commands a dramatic vista of the City and surrounding countryside. One writer describing Prior Park has said "The natural beauties of wood, water, and prospect, hill and dale, wilderness and cultivation, makes it one of the most delightful spots I ever saw". In the Medieval Period here was situated the country seat of the Prior of Bath Abbey, whose residence was not on the slope of the present mansion, but farther down the valley and nearer the well-stocked fish-ponds. Its name indicates the ancient owners of the land – the Priors of Bath Abbey, from whom, at the dissolution of the monasteries, it was taken and granted to one Humphrey Colles, who quickly disposed of it to Matthew Colthurst. His son Edmund presented the Abbey Church, which was then in a ruinous condition, having been stripped of its lead, glass, and bells, to the Mayor and citizens of Bath for their parish church. He then sold the Abbey House together with the Prior Park estate to a Fulk Morley from whose descendants it passed through the Duke of Kingston, to Lord Newark, to be finally purchased by Ralph Allen, an innkeeper's son from Cornwall, who by introducing the cross-country system, made a fortune from pulling the postal services out of the chaos created by letters being routed through London.

Ralph Allen was now set to make his second fortune, and in 1726 he purchased the Combe Down Estates, and the opening of the quarries soon followed. Bath was burgeoning, it was already the success story of the 18th century, assisted no doubt by the steps taken to make the River Avon navigable for barge traffic between Bath and Bristol, by introducing a series of locks and bridges which made it possible for Bath stone to be sent down river to Bristol, and timber and other materials from Bristol to come upstream. The businesslike sagacity displayed by Ralph Allen, as indeed in all other matters again came to the forefront, and in 1730 Allen purchased Bathampton Down, where stone quarrying developed on similar lines to

The North Front, Prior Park

Combe Down. He now set himself the task of devising means for carrying the stone to the riverside, and not lacking in originality, an ingenious scheme was arranged whereby the stone was conveyed on wooden rails down what is now Ralph Allen Drive, propelled by the forces of gravity to the wharfside, where after unloading, horses would be hitched to the wagons to haul them up the hill again. Orders for Bath Stone crowded in on Allen from all quarters. He was cheaper than anyone else, and at times it was difficult for his organisation to meet the demand and more difficult still to find ways and means to make the shipment.

Allen by now was the manorial lord of Bathampton and Claverton, and as Squire Allen and a patron of the arts he wanted to create his own Elysium to which his friends could come and be entertained in a variety of ways, in a setting that conjured up his many moods, and so in 1735 the building of Prior Park commenced. There was a slight set-back early in 1736 when the first Mrs. Allen died, but on marrying Elizabeth Holder in 1737 building continued with renewed vigour.

Prior Park was built in the Palladian style, which was at the time being vigorously revived under the influence of Richard Boyle, 3rd Earl of Burlington, whose own villa at Chiswick was possibly the most influential Neo-Palladian building in England. The mansions of the wealthy landowners, to be considered fashionable and up-to-date, were being pulled down or altered to conform to the new style. John Wood was fortunate, as the architect of Prior Park and consulting advisor to Allen, he had virgin country in which to set his masterpiece. He describes the magnificent portico on the north side as the grand pavilion, which was never used as an entrance. Stone balustrades were placed as a protection in the interstices of the columns, and no

71

doubt Allen's fascinating circle of friends and acquaintances, among them Pope, Quin, Fielding, Pitt the Elder (The Great Commoner), Smollett, and many others, used it as a belvedere where they enjoyed the cooling breezes, and the splendid views of the distant City.

Wood's plan provided for a central residential mansion, with almost identical wings containing the dairies, stabling, and servant's quarters, on each side of the house. On the northern aspect he built in the Corinthian style upon a rustic basement storey, the centre part of which projected from the plane to form one of the most correct and noble porticos in England. Nicholas Pevsner refers to it as "The most ambitious and most complete recreation of Palladio's villas on English soil" (page 114 "The Buildings of England", North Somerset edition.) Wood's piquancy comes to the forefront in his treatment of the entrance side, where he "rings the changes" by introducing the Ionic order in the entrance front. This variation of orders, Ionic or

Mansion Chapel

Corinthian, is introduced again in his original decor for the rooms inside the house. Wood, unfortunately, did not live to see the completion of Prior Park, he died in 1754, and Richard Jones, who was Wood's clerk of works completed the building. The Palladian bridge over the fishponds at the foot of the estate was built about 1755 and is a copy of the famous bridge which spans the River Nadder at Wilton House which was designed by Roger Morris. There is a slight difference in design however, the gallery of Wilton's bridge carries a coffered ceiling, whereas at Prior Park the ceiling is simply treated with plain plastering.

One interesting feature which remains as it was when built, is the chapel which completed most of the mansion's eastern end, and which was, according to John Wood, included in the main building to enable Allen and his guests to attend divine service as the nearest parish church was some distance away. Here is displayed the vision of one architect's conception of the classical orders, in the treatment of the two tiers of columns and pilasters, Corinthian above and Ionic below, which decorate the altar end and the galleried end opposite.

The country house of the 18th century took on a new role. The wealth of the great landowners and entrepreneurs was considerable, and they vied with each other in their opulent display of wealth. They could not hang their money bags around their necks, but they could build these magnificent and splendidly sited houses within artificially constructed landscapes of vistas, water, trees, temples, and statues. This was partly true of Allen's reason for building Prior Park, but he did have an "axe to grind", and there is little doubt that the real motive was to overcome the prejudice against the Bath freestone, which led to its rejection by Colen Campbell, and to Allen's tender for the supply of stone for the building of Greenwich Hospital.

Ralph Allen died in the summer of 1764, and was buried in the churchyard at Claverton where his friend Richard Green was rector. If the desire to promote the arts and entertain his many friends were the dominant influences on Ralph Allen in building Prior Park, he succeeded, but somehow when he died Prior Park died with him, and it was never the same, for within two years of his death Mrs Allen died childless, and as Allen's only son had already died the inheritance passed into the possession of Bishop Warburton, who had married Allen's niece, Gertrude Tucker, and on her death in 1796, it came, under the will of Ralph Allen, into the possession of Mary, daughter of Allen's brother Philip. Mary Allen had married Cornwallis Maude who in 1785 was made Baron de Montalt, and later to become Viscount Hawarden. Hawarden tried to revive the fortunes of Prior Park, but on his death and that of his son who died childless it would seem that the Allen influence at Prior Park terminated.

The property passed then by purchase to Chandler Browne, and then to John Thomas, a Quaker, of Bristol who became actively concerned with the Kennet and Avon Canal. He is commemorated by having an inscribed plaque on the Dundas Aqueduct at Limpley Stoke.

In December 1829 Prior Park was purchased for the purpose of a Catholic Theological College by Bishop Baines, for the sum of £22000. Until now Prior Park remained substantially unaltered, apart from the removal of its original furnishings, and other removable decorative features which followed soon after the death of Ralph Allen. The Baines era brought many changes, the east and west wings were entirely reconstructed to provide additional accommodation for Prior Park College, and Henry Goodridge was commissioned to design the fine staircase leading down from the northern portico to the lower terraces, to become the most striking feature of the northern aspect

After the fire of May 29th 1836 which almost gutted the building, the remodelling and restoration of the whole fabric became a dedication. Fortunately at that time, Hunstrete House near Marksbury, a fine mansion built by Francis Popham of Littlecote, was being dismantled, and much of the plasterwork and chimney pieces, together with the doors and doorcases, which were in many ways attractive examples of 18th century work, found their way to Prior Park.

Decline once more threatened Prior Park; Bishop Baines died in 1843, and this sparked off a succession of difficulties, culminating in the closing of the college in 1856, and the property was immediately offered for sale by public auction. For many years the property remained in an uncared for condition. At that time the tenant was a benevolent individual by the name of Thompson who turned the parkland into, to use the modern vernacular, a picnic area.

For ten years or more Prior Park remained in the hands of mortgagees, until Bishop Doctor Clifford of Clifton, using much of his personal wealth re-purchased the estate for the sum of £23000 in 1867. With the help of many benefactors Prior Park made great steps towards recovery as a Catholic College. One important event was the building and completion of the Church of St. Paul in the western wing. Designed by Joseph Scoles many years earlier it was completed by his son Alexander Scoles in 1882.

Adversity was never far removed and with the death of Doctor Clifford in 1893 the school's fortunes were again in decline, until in 1904 it finally closed. From then on it was used in various ways until 1924 when the Christian Brothers bought the property and once again it became a school. Even Hitler's air attack on Bath in 1942 left its mark on Prior Park, considerable damage was done which made the buildings useless for a while.

The post war years have at long last brought a burgeoning success to Prior Park. With help from the Ministry of Public Buildings and Works (now included in the Department of the Environment), and the Pilgrims Trust by way of grants, a considerable amount of restoration has been carried out. To stand on Goodridge's staircase and take in the panoramic vista of Bath is one of the joys of this world. As one man succinctly described Prior Park, "A noble building which sees all Bath, and which was built for all Bath to see".

Ralph Allen's Town House York Street, Bath

Buchanan speaking seriously of its restoration said, "This neglected building, needs cleaning up, and could be turned into a tourist attraction, possibly opening up the interior to form a series of connected galleries for a museum or exhibition space. The key would be in buying and demolishing the small shop at 7a York Street, and this in turn could lead to a paved walk." Well at least one of Buchanan's thoughts have come to fruition. A most satisfying scheme of restoration has been completed almost on lines suggested by the Professor, although at the present time the future use of interior is uncertain. Perhaps there is no house in Bath which is located in a more hidden and out-of-the-way situation. The entrance to the little courtyard lies between the Friend's Meeting House in York Street, and a small shop which has been rebuilt so as to make way for the fine gateway entrance just as Buchanan suggested.

The house originally bordered Liliput Alley, known formerly as Segar's Alley or Evelyn Street, but now renamed North Parade Passage, and it had at one time a pleasant sloping garden in front, and a wide open view of Bathampton Down beyond, upon which Allen built later his whimsy "Sham Castle". After Allen's removal to Prior Park, the garden was gradually encroached upon, and this delightful house was almost hidden from view.

The north wing was added in 1727, with its principal front, the garden front, facing east. The design as well as the model for additions to Allen's house were made while John Wood was in London in the early part of 1727, and later writing in his "Description of Bath" John Wood had this to say. "While Mr. Allen was making the Addition to the North Part of his House in Lilliput Alley, he new fronted and raised the old Building a full Storey higher; and this is surmounted by an Attick, which created a sixth Rate House, and a Sample for the greatest Magnificence that was ever proposed by me for our City Houses."

For the first time in many years it is now possible to appreciate the architectural skills of John Wood's "elaborate Palladian frontispiece"

Ralph Allen's Town House

(Walter Ison's description in his "The Georgian Buildings of Bath"). The east front presents an elegant facade, consisting of a rusticated base supporting four engaged three-quarter columns, having moulded bases on plain pedestals, plain shafts, and Corinthian capitals, which divide the front into three bays. The whole supporting a most elaborately carved pediment.

It was in this house, when it possessed the right and left wings, that Allen, besides using it as his private residence, carried on the business as postmaster and his cross-posts enterprise. For in 1720 Allen offered the government of the day £6000 a year for the rights to run England's country post. His offer was accepted, and Allen pulled the country postal service out of the chaos caused by all letters being routed through London, and before long most towns of note were linked by a six-days-a-week cross country system. Ralph Allen was making a profit of £12000 a year from this venture, which was a considerable fortune in the early 18th century. The ghost of Ralph Allen must surely have fallen about with laughter at the discomfiture of the 20th century Post Office in its failure to make the postal system pay. He became a member of the Bath Corporation in 1722, and became mayor in 1742 where his influence was such that he was referred to as the "The One-headed Corporation".

Right up to 1785 the house was still in use for postal business, but after Allen's death in 1764, it fell into a state of decay from sheer neglect. The north wing was removed to make way for the building of York Street in the 19th century. It is sad when a fine house falls on hard times, having witnessed the gaiety of beautifully dressed women, splendidly attired men in military uniforms and of rakish cut clothes, competing with each other, but all enjoying the generous hospitality of this "Man of Bath" – and then silence.

St. Catherine's Court
Batheaston, Near Bath

Leave the high decibel count of the traffic in Batheaston High Street, and take the lane through Northend village to St. Catherine, a small hamlet still dominated by its old manor house and nearby church. After leaving Northend the approach to this delightful backwater is made through a winding, uneven lane which snakes its way up and down the hillside between high-banked hedges, which give way at intervals to offer superb views of the valley climbing towards the highway from Bath to Gloucester. Survival of the countryside is one of my recurring themes, and it is heart warming to see here that no one has made the irretrievable mistake of sacrificing natural beauty for material gain.

St. Catherine's is a remarkable house, a small manorial home, with considerable interest to students of the 15th century. Built on the carcass of the old monastic buildings of Prior Cantlow of Bath Abbey who came here some 500 years ago, what is seen today date from the Tudor and early Jacobean periods with some modern additions. The manor belonged to the Priors of Bath from very early times, and it is said that the monks would row up the Avon in their barges as far as Bathford, whence they made their way up the valley to St. Catherine's.

At the time of the dissolution the lease of the Manor was held by one Thomas Llewellyn, Collector of Rents of Batheaston and St. Catherine's, who continued in this office until 1546. "The Dictionary of National Biography" had this to say about the next owners:

John Harington seems to have been a confidential servant of Henry VIII, and revived his fortunes by marrying the illegitimate daughter of the king, known as Etheldreda or sometimes as Audry, the daughter of Joanna Dyngley. She was brought up by Henry's tailor, John Malte, as a natural daughter of his own. Henry granted Etheldreda the monastic forfeitures of Kelston, Batheaston, and Katherine in Somerset, and on his marriage in 1546 Harington settled down at

St Catherine's Court

Kelston on his wife's estates. Etheldreda soon died without issue leaving her lands to her husband, who showed his gratitude to his benefactor by devoting himself to the services of the Princess Elizabeth. He eventually married Elizabeth Markham a lady-in-waiting to the Princess in 1554, and when a son John was born, the Princess acted as his godmother. The son became Sir John Harington and it has been said that he was compelled to sell St. Catherine's to meet the heavy expenditure incurred by entertaining Queen Elizabeth at Kelston.

The property was then leased to John Blanchard of Marshfield, a wealthy woolmaster. He paid £1250 and a rent of £20 a year, and 'two couples of capons". John was followed by his son William Blanchard, in which family the Court remained for several generations. It passed then into the possession of James Walters of Batheaston, until an heiress brought the property into the family of Parry. The manor then passed through several families until in 1841 it became the property of a Colonel Joseph Holden Strutt, M.P. for the Maldon division of Essex, and great grandfather of the late Major Geoffrey St. John Strutt, the last member of this family to live there.

The Strutts were appreciative owners, carrying out many improvements to the house, and restoring the nearby church. On Colonel Strutt's death in 1845, at the age of 87, the Court passed to his youngest daughter Charlotte Olivia, wife of the Rev. Robert Drummond, and remained in her ownership until 1897. Richard Strutt became the next owner in 1912, and further additions were made to the buildings. He built the library, added the orangery, and improved further the gardens constructed earlier by the Blanchards.

He made considerable alterations to the interior, paying particular attention to the large drawing room, where the ugly Victorian decor was replaced by the more elegant style of the late 17th century in the treatment of the wall panelling, and the plasterwork of the ceiling. The library is in the east end of the south front, and is contained in an entirely new building with the orangery just below. The library ceiling and woodwork are again imitations of the Jacobean style.

On the death of Richard Strutt the Court passed to his second son Geoffrey St. John Strutt who opened his house once a week to visitors. On his death the house was closed.

In 1975 new owners occupied the Court, they were the St. Catherine's Trust, an inter-denominational body formed to promote the Christian way of life and community service who paid £70000 for the manor. The inspiration behind this purchase was to create a residential home for students, but it did seem to meet with local opposition. It is easy to understand their objection to what appeared to be a worthwhile enterprise. No doubt by looking into the future they could see the tranquillity and beauty of this valley being threatened by the intrusion of the motor car, and so the plan was turned down by the planning authority. However all is not lost, for the historian Katherine Christopher has recently purchased the Court and plans to spend time and money on restoring it to its pristine state.

One of the greatest assets of St. Catherine's Court was its matchless garden. The first William Blanchard over three centuries ago tamed the precipitous garden slopes, constructed eye-catching terraces and a mighty yew-hedge, one of the finest in this part of the West Country. Alas, the gardens today have been sadly neglected, perhaps in caring hands they could be reclaimed and restored to offer once more their gorgeous riot of climbing roses, delphiniums, sweet williams, and a grand assortment of Old English flowers.

Standing within the grounds of the Court is the ancient church, largely the creation of Prior Cantlow. He pulled down the Norman church and set about constructing an English one. It is a charming place, showing evidence of the Benedictine monks who helped to build it. In the stained glass in the east window over the altar the Arms of Bath Priory are displayed, with the following inscription:

"Dni Johnis Cantlow, quonda prior is hanc cacella fieri fecit ao. Dui MCCCCLXXXXIX."

To the left of the altar there is a splendid monument to William Blanchard who died in 1631. He is clothed in the half armour of Charles's time, and behind him kneels his wife, in a long bleak flowing gown and wearing a kind of wimple round her head. On the pediment are three daughters kneeling in a row, with the son kneeling at a reading desk. There is a fine wooden pulpit, the Gothic niches of which are picked out in red and yellow, and which still retain almost the brightness of the original colourings. Here is material for a calm contemplation by anyone who relishes the good things of country life.

Stourhead
Wilts

The area covered by Stourhead was once part of the Forest of Selwood, and here on its southern edge the Norman henchmen of William cleared the forest and created their estates. The identity of the original owner is a little obscure, but it is almost certain that the Stourton family were living here long before the 15th century, for in 1448 Sir John Stourton, a former High Sheriff of Wiltshire, was created the first Lord Stourton by Henry VI.

A descendant of the first Lord Stourton came to an untimely end in Salisbury market place, he was the eighth Lord, and was publicly hanged for the murder of two men, father and son, by the name of Hartgill, workers on his vast estate. The two were seeking better conditions of employment from their lord and master, a retrograde step to make in those unenlightened days, this enraged the peppery nobleman to a point where he lost control of his actions.

However little more was heard regarding the whole sordid episode, the Stourtons managed to retain their estates until 1714 when the thirteenth Lord sold the property to Sir John Meres of Kirkby Bellars in Leicester, who later sold in 1720 the whole of the former Stourton estate to Henry Hoare, son of Sir Richard Hoare, former Lord Mayor of London, and founder of Hoare's Bank.

Changes were soon to take place, Henry Hoare pulled down Old Stourton House and built a new one in a completely different style on another site. It was the generation of Burlington, Kent, and Campbell, architects who witnessed the rejection of the baroque and rococo, and their replacement by a new style – Neo Classicism – that depended on strict imitation of the Greek orders. The Scottish born architect Colen Campbell was consulted by Henry Hoare, and Stourton House, now renamed Stourhead by Hoare, illustrates the regular, restrained in ornament, style according to the classical rules initiated into England by Inigo Jones one hundred years earlier.

Henry Hoare never saw the completed mansion, he died in 1725, and it was left to his son Henry junior to complete the interior, and

The East Front, Stourhead

Temple and Lake, Stourhead

the landscaping of the parkland. He employed another architect, Henry Flitcroft, to design the temples, copies of the Greek originals, which fitted so successfully into the landscaping, and added to the scene the romantic touch. Flitcroft also created the massive lake by damming a valley to the west of the house containing the headwaters of the River Stour. Today the gardens at Stourhead exemplify the best in the changing style of 18th century landscaping, and Henry Hoare junior accomplished this without any assistance from Capability Brown, the recognised master of all 18th century landscape gardeners. Horace Walpole referring to the Stourhead landscape wrote in 1762, "one of the most picturesque scenes in the world".

Two years before his death in 1785, Henry made over the estate to his grandson Richard Colt Hoare. Henry's daughter had married her cousin Sir Richard Hoare, first Baronet, and Richard Colt Hoare succeeded as second Baronet in 1787. The second Sir Richard was soon to become equally famous as a successful antiquary, county historian, and dilettante. To house his library and collection of paintings he added a pair of wings to the house during the period from 1796 to 1800. Colt Hoare followed the fashion of that time by purchasing paintings by Continental artists. Works by Carlo Maratta, Cigoli, Nicolas and Gaspard Poussin were represented, and also on view today is a collection of pictures by the Swiss artist Louis Ducros. The British school is well represented, and the display includes some small scale sculptures by Rysbrack. There are good examples of furniture of the Georgian and later periods, including some outstanding work by Thomas Chippendale.

The Pantheon, Stourhead

As an archaeologist and county historian Colt Hoare visited and excavated close on 400 Wiltshire barrows. On one occasion during a disagreement with his fellow antiquarian Pitt-Rivers he was accused of disposing of his skeletons far too quickly, Hoare riposted "it grinned horribly, a ghastly smile, a singularity I have never before noticed". Nevertheless no better tribute could be given to this undoubted scholar than the honour of having his effigy seated on one of the Stourhead library chairs in Salisbury Cathedral.

Sir Richard Colt Hoare's half-brother Sir Henry Hugh Hoare succeeded to the property and titles to become the third Baronet in 1838, and it was this member of the family who completed Colen Campbell's original design for the east front by adding the portico in 1840, until then the east front displayed an engaged portico.

Sir Henry was followed by his son Sir Hugh Richard Hoare, who became the fourth Baronet. He died in 1857 and a nephew Sir Henry Ainsley Hoare succeeded and became the fifth Baronet. In 1894 Sir Henry Hugh Arthur Hoare became the sixth Baronet, and lived at Stourhead for fifty-three years. During this period, in 1902 to be precise, the centre block of the mansion was destroyed by fire, although most of the contents were saved. Rebuilding was commenced almost immediately, and Sir Henry engaged Sir Aston Webb and Dorian Webb to supervise the rebuilding. The west front which collapsed after the fire is built quite differently from Campbell's austerity treatment for the east front, and the change is no improvement. Fortunately the east front survived the fire.

In 1946 Sir Henry gave Stourhead and its contents, and 2300 acres to the National Trust. His only son had died of wounds in 1917 and he had no direct heir. In March of 1947 Sir Henry died on the same day as his wife. They both left to posterity a grand house and magnificent gardens second to none, owed to the genius of the Hoare family who created it.

Credit must be given to the gardener Henry for the building of the brick landmark, known as Alfred's Tower. It is supposed to mark the spot where King Alfred set up his camp before his victory over the Danes at Ethandune in 879.

Thomas Gainsborough's House 17 The Circus, Bath

The Circus has had from time to time many noted residents, but perhaps none more distinguished than Thomas Gainsborough, the son of John Gainsborough a cloth merchant, who was born at Sudbury in Suffolk in 1727. Very early he showed signs of artistic genius, and it was his early efforts at landscape painting that persuaded his father to give way and allow his son to go to London to study. By the time he was thirteen he became a pupil and eventually assistant to the French engraver Hubert Gravelot, but his real talents were not recognised until he settled in Bath. The irascible Philip Thicknesse, his biographer and patron said of him 'Of all the men I ever knew, he possessed least of all, worldly knowledge". Well he had the sense to move to Bath which at that time was the favourite resort of the wealthy, the privilege, and the fashionable. He had previously married at the age of 19 an illegitimate daughter of the Duke of Beaufort, one Margaret Burr, who was in receipt of an annuity of £200 per annum, a useful sum and a considerable comfort to a young painter in those days.

Arriving in Bath in 1758 he started to paint portraits at five guineas a time, and with growing success he was able to increase this to eight. Commissions were now forthcoming and he decided to move from his indifferent studio in the Abbey Churchyard to the more elegant surroundings of the Circus. He always considered himself a landscape painter, but the need for hard cash forced him to paint portraits, a situation he never took kindly to, and later on in life when he was considering retirement, he wrote to Sir William Chambers at the Royal Academy saying, "If I can pick pockets in the portrait way two or three years longer I intend to sneak away and turn into a serious fellow". He never did retire.

During the period he lived in the Circus he produced some of his most famous paintings, and from time to time he was able to show his work in the Pump Room, which attracted considerable attention from the more wealthy of Bath society. His full length pictures rose in value

Gainsborough House, The Circus

from £50 to as much as £100. It was whilst here that his paintings of Elizabeth Linley, Richard Sheridan, Edmund Burke, Garrick, Quin, and many others were executed. On one occasion when he heard that his portraits of Foote and Garrick were not considered good likenesses, he riposted, "Rot them for a couple of rogues, they have everybody's faces but their own".

Gainsborough enjoyed living in Bath where he had numerous friends, including the cult figure Doctor Samuel Johnson, whose "circle" would meet in the Pelican Inn in Walcot Street, preferring "this quiet hostelry, with its capacious courtyard and pleasant garden" to the resorts of the wealthy and fashionable. Here he would meet Joshua Reynolds, Garrick, Quin, and Sheridan. The Pelican later renamed the Three Cups has now disappeared to make way for the car park. It is interesting to know at that time Walcot Street was considered a fashionable thoroughfare, and the siting of the inn furnished its guests with the dubious opportunity of watching the "quality" that passed in their sedan chairs.

In 1774 Gainsborough had good reason to leave Bath and moved to London. The Royal Academy had been set up six years earlier by George III, and which now gave greater opportunities to artists to show their works and to enhance their reputations. Gainsborough previously had became a founder member, and with his friend and

85

contemporary Sir Joshua Reynolds holding the exalted position of being elected the first President, he felt isolated in Bath. He moved to Schomberg House in Pall Mall, part of which still stands today, and he lived there until his death in 1788. Sir Joshua Reynolds said of him "We have lately lost Mr. Gainsborough, one of the greatest ornaments of our Academy".

At the time of Gainsborough's departure from Bath, more people than ever were coming to the city. The influx grew with the building of the turnpike roads and the introduction in 1784 of fast mail coaches, the inspiration of John Palmer, the son of the manager of the Bath and Bristol theatres, whose coaches reduced the journey from London to Bath down to fifteen hours.

The new residents of the Circus were the half-pay officers, and retired naval men, prosperous clothiers, and ecclesiastics, who found that living in Bath was cheaper than in London. John Wood the Younger had just completed the new or Upper Assembly Rooms and the fashionable society of the City began to desert the Lower Rooms, where Nash's elaborate system of punctilio was already in decay, for the more informal etiquette of the New Rooms.

Both the Woods, father and son, were involved in the building of the Circus, both were architects of national stature, and because of their influence Bath gave the lead in Palladian town architecture. Their treatment of the elegant facades to the houses in the Circus displays with considerable emphasis, their exclusive adherence to the classical orders.

The Town Houses of Richard "Beau" Nash Bath

"Thomas Greenway began another Court of Houses on the Town Mixen (Dung-heap), upon the West Side of the Timber Green (Sawclose), to which he gave the name of St. John's Court. Part of the first house that was built in it became the Palace of the King of Bath (Beau Nash), and it was the richest sample of building, till then executed, in the City." This was John Wood in his "Essay towards a Description of Bath", succinctly describing Beau Nash's houses in St. John's Court. The house on the corner of the court and Sawclose was without doubt the most imposing residence in Bath, and had it been in London it could well have been the town house of some aristocrat or ambassador. It brings into focus the sheer magnitude of Nash's personality, his genius, and his stupidity.

Richard "Beau" Nash was born in 1674, a son of an unsuccessful Swansea glass manufacturer. Educated at Carmarthen Grammar School, from where he went up to Jesus College, Oxford in 1691. He had to leave Oxford hurriedly without taking a degree, as a result of his personal proclivities with a local girl. He made his way to London where he managed to join the Guards as an ensign, but it soon became abundantly clear that he was quite unsuited to this kind of discipline, and so he turned to the legal profession where his talents for dressing, eating well, and gambling were well rewarded, earning for himself the nickname of the "Count". In 1695 he was chosen to organise a pageant to celebrate the accession of William III, and the production so impressed the King that he offered Nash a knighthood, which Nash refused, saying that he would have preferred to have been made a "poor Knight of Windsor", which would have carried a pension.

In 1705 Nash's fortunes were at a low ebb, and in this impecunious state he drifted to Bath, which at that time teemed with fashionable society following the visit of Queen Anne to the city earlier. It was not long before his plausible manner came to the notice of Captain Webster, the reigning Master of Ceremonies, who made him his social assistant. When later Webster was killed in a duel over cheating at cards, his post was offered to Nash, and so started a reign that was to last for over half a century.

Nash's influence persuaded the Corporation to build a Pump Room, thus enabling "patients" to drink the ritual glass of lukewarm beverage in comfort. Nash went further and introduced the reading of newspapers and magazines accompanied by musicians playing in the gallery. He became a force in civilising Georgian Society and created an elaborate system of public punctilio. Meanwhile his own fortunes were not without success, the house in St. John's Court had been filled with a unique collection of furniture, the reception rooms gleamed with crystal and gold, and Nash's lifestyle was by now an extravagance. He was also a compulsive gambler and womaniser, and it was not long before a mistress was installed at St. John's Court, by the name of Fanny Murray. Fanny was part of the flotsam and jetsam thrown up in the streets of London in the 18th century. At the age of 12 this ragged child was begging on the steps of the Covent Garden Theatre, when she was approached by Jack Spencer, a notorious rake, and a grandson of the Duchess of Marlborough. Poor Fanny, she fell for the veneer of old fashioned charm and was seduced by Jack on the steps of the theatre. Spencer was so intrigued with Fanny that he took her to live with him, but faithfulness was not one of Fanny's virtues and eventually she joined Nash in Bath to share his bed at St. John's Court. Her charms and voluptuousness inspired John Wilkes to write his famous "Essay on Woman".

Tongues began to wag, and on one occasion Nash was branded as a whoremonger by a local gossip, he demanded an explanation from his accuser, "I've been informed it is true." "Then," replied Nash, "you are misinformed, I acknowledge I have a woman living in my house, but if I do keep her a man can no more be termed a whoremonger for having one whore in the house than a cheesemonger for having one cheese." It was one angry moment on the part of Nash in an otherwise urbane performance.

Nash's affluence kept pace with Bath's progress, and although no one really knew the source of his wealth, it was suspected that he was getting a fair rake off from the gaming houses in the City. Nash's vanity was plainly shewn in the way he would drive in state through the City in a gilded coach pulled by six black horses, and driven by a coachman and an assistant, a postillion with two footmen would stand at the rear. In addition there would be outriders blowing on horns during their journey around the City, and the great "Beau" would lean out and wave a languid hand to the admiring crowds.

Nash was not a great man in the sense that he could serve as an inspiration or a model, he was no colossus, yet many who found some of his ideas preposterous and his pretensions dubious to say the least were subdued into awe by the force of his personality. Of course there was the incident of John Wesley's visit to the City in 1739 when he had an encounter with Beau Nash in Avon Street. Wesley was

Richard 'Beau' Nash's House,
Sawclose

preaching to a large crowd which was joined by Nash who immediately took Wesley to task, telling him he was acting contrary to law. "Besides," Nash said "your preaching frightens people out of their wits." "Sir," said Wesley, "did you ever hear me preach?" "No," said Nash. "Then how can you judge of what you never heard?" "By common report," Nash said stoutly. "Common report is not enough. Is not your name Nash?" "My name is Nash." "Sir," replied Wesley, "I dare not judge of you by common report." The rebuff went home.

Nash was always conscious about his obscure parentage, and on one occasion when the Duchess of Marlborough was particularly mordacious, Nash quipped characteristically, "Madam, I seldom mention my father in company, not because I have any reason to be ashamed of him, but because he has some reason to be ashamed of me."

Various acts of Parliament regarding the gaming laws passed between 1739 and 1745 narrowed the profits to be made. Nash suffered a considerable financial loss, aggravated further by an unsuccessful legal battle, which forced him to move from St. John's Court to a smaller house a short distance away, and which is now a restaurant named after Juliana Popjoy, Nash's last mistress. It was here that Nash now quite old and impoverished died on February 3rd 1761 aged 87, and all Bath mourned. A small marble tablet on the house indicates his having lived and died there. The City Corporation, not over generous, voted the sum of £50 towards the funeral expenses, and he was buried with some amount of pomp on February 8th in the Abbey where a tablet bears an inscription by Doctor Harington.

Nash's last house is well preserved both externally and internally, and remains a fine example of Thomas Greenway's earlier building. The house consists of two stories and a roof attic, but its most distinguishing feature is the entrance door so often missed by the casual passer by. The doorway displays two Corinthian columns supporting an entablature bearing two pedestals with eagles perched on half spheres.

Nash's first house must have made an impressive corner site before the Theatre Royal excrescence was grafted on to it, and much of the fine interior disappeared when the rear portion became the Garrick's Head, but it is gratifying to see that part of the exterior has been restored by the new owners of the Theatre. This house was built in 1720, and Wood never at a loss to under-estimate Thomas Greenway's qualities, criticises the house for profuse ornament which is typical of a mason and not an architect.

No. 5 Trim Street Bath

Trim Street derives its name from George Trim, a wealthy clothier of Bath, and member of the City Corporation. His mother apparently was related to Inigo Jones. Trim Street was one of the first streets to be built outside the old city walls, and dates from the year 1707. Number 5 which is often referred to as "Wolfe's House", and until quite recently used as offices by the British Gas Corporation, is on the north side adjoining St. John's Gate, perhaps better known as "Trim Bridge".

James Wolfe was born and brought up in Westerham in Kent. His birth actually took place in the vicarage, but most of his early life before entering the army at the early age of 14 was spent at Spiers, now called Quebec House. He fought in the War of the Austrian Succession alongside George II, the last English king to lead his troops, at the battle of Dettingen. He followed General Wade in his pacification of the Highlands, and became a staff officer at Culloden, and finally though barely 22 years of age he had achieved by his own merit the rank of lieutenant-colonel.

In 1757 Wolfe's parents were living at No. 5. Trim Street, and during their stay here Wolfe, broken down in health, joined them. During this period he met a Miss Lowther, the daughter of Robert Lowther one time Governor of Barbados, but because of Wolfe's dedication to his profession, this romance which at the best of times was always difficult never came to fruition. Whilst in Bath he wrote constantly of reform in the army, and his disquiet over certain military setbacks overseas compelled him to write, "We are the most egregious blunderers in war that ever took the hatchet in hand".

This outburst did not prevent William Pitt from dispatching him to North America, where the Marquis of Montcalm had scored many successes against the British forces there. So Wolfe a young soldier of thirty-three was summoned from Bath by Pitt, and given orders to lead the British army against the French in Canada. In 1759 he arrived and took up his appointment, but it was only after many delays that he finally came face to face with the French before

General James Wolfe's House, No. 5
Trim Street

Quebec after completing the almost impossible task of taking the British army up the Heights of Abraham. In the moment of victory Wolfe was hit in the breast by a musket ball and died later.

It is uncertain who designed No. 5, but the general treatment and the detail seem to point to the architect Thomas Greenway. The arms trophy contained in the pediment over the entrance is a later addition, said to be a memorial to Wolfe, and was designed by Prince Hoare son of a local painter.

Wade's House
Abbey Churchyard, Bath

Bring back to life and preserve the historic buildings of Bath, not as museums, but as updated buildings, fulfilling a modern and useful function. How many times has this been said in the City over the last decade? Well Marshal Wade's House at No. 14 Abbey Churchyard has been made to fulfil that role. The house, formerly part of the premises occupied by Cyril Howe Ltd, the photographic firm, has been purchased by the Landmark Trust. Basically this is a charitable organisation having as its main object, the purchase, and making use of old buildings, by converting them into flats, offices, and up-to-date holiday homes, but at the same time ensuring there is no loss of their original charm and antiquity. The Landmark Trust has achieved its object in the painstaking restoration carried out on Wade's old house. The two top floors have been converted into a self-contained holiday flat, and the National Trust occupies the ground and first floors for use as a shop and a Trust information centre.

The National Trust, never backward in promoting its image, and certainly never at a loss to swell its funds, has been in the gift business for many years, and so in the tastefully fitted shop which occupies the ground floor of the house, the Trust has provided for itself the most distinguished site in Bath.

Marshal Wade who resided here from 1720 until his death in 1748 descended from Sir William Wade who had so leading a part in the colonisation of Virginia, and later as Lieutenant-Governor of the Tower of London earned for himself the epithet of "that villian Wade", from his prisoner Sir Walter Raleigh. Another ancestor was Colonel Nathaniel Wade, the ill-fated Monmonth's companion at Sedgemoor, and the man who fired the fatal pistol shot at night which roused the king's troops in their bivouacs near Westonzoyland, and of course there was Sir Claude Wade K.C.B. who first forced the Khyber Pass, and who died rather quietly at his Bath home No. 16 Queen Square.

Bath's Marshal Wade was elected Member of Parliament for the City in 1722, and continued to represent Bath until his death, but his real claim to fame was the construction of the military roads in Scotland, and the disarming of the Highland clans. Not for nothing did Englishmen sing:

> "God grant General Wade
>   May by thy Almighty aid,
> Victory bring. May he sedition hush
>   And like a torrent rush
> Rebellious Scots to crush,
>   God save the King"

Wade was Ralph Allen's staunch friend, and in Allen's early years his patron. All this came about from an act of zeal on the part of Allen whilst employed as a Post Office clerk in Bath. The Old Pretender had many friends in and around Bath, and it did not take long for the astute Allen to latch on as to what was going on from the mail passing through his office, and his suspicions were conveyed to Marshal Wade. For this service Allen obtained the offices of Postmaster at Bath, and shortly afterwards married Miss Earle, Wade's illegitimate daughter.

Wade had one weakness, he had a great passion for gaming, it has been said that this was his reason for living in Bath where he could indulge as frequently as he pleased, in fact he built his house in the City so that he could live here and enjoy its peachy environment. The house now facing into Abbey Churchyard was much larger, and when first built, its northern facade faced Cheap Street, at that time a narrow passage only a few feet in width. Later in the 18th century because of Bath's street improvement schemes, Cheap Street was widened which meant the ornate front of Wade's House was removed, and an attic storey was added which in no way improved the elevation.

The southern front became the main entrance, and the four bay ground storey, which provided a base supporting five Ionic pilasters, was later replaced by a fine Regency shop-front. Credit for the design of this house has been given to Richard Boyle, third Earl of Burlington, amateur architect and patron of the arts. There is little evidence to support this, and the ascription to the noble earl is based on the fact that he designed Wade's London residence. This house – the London house – had so grand a front, that Lord Chesterfield was induced to remark, "As the General could not live in it at his ease, he had better take a house opposite and look at it".

One cannot dismiss Richard Boyle's connection with the Wades completely. The Boyle's family connection with Somerset goes back to 1649, when Roger Boyle, the first Earl of Orrery, horrified by the execution of Charles I quitted Ireland and lived in strict retirement at Marston Park near Frome. The Boyles as a family were devotees of the arts and sciences, but perhaps of all the members of this erudite family, Richard Boyle the third earl was the most distinguished. He is celebrated for his architectural tastes, and his friendship with artists

Marshall Wade's House

and the literati. His fortune was considerable and his generosity outstanding. "Never," wrote Horace Walpole, "was protection and great wealth more generously and more judiciously diffused than by this great person, who had every quality of a genius and an artist, except envy." Perhaps after all there may be some substance in his connection with Wade's Bath house. The Boyle family severed their connection with Somerset in 1905, when they sold Marston House with several farms to a Mr. Fletcher of Tisbury.

Wade was a great benefactor of the City, he built the alley formerly called "Wade's Passage' as a convenient "communication between the walks and the pump", prior to this the houses adjoining the Abbey on the north side prevented any use of a "common footway". Marshal Wade left a considerable fortune when he died, and a sum of £500 was set aside for the erection of a monument to himself, either in Bath Abbey or Westminster Abbey. The latter was chosen, and a bust was placed over the Canon's door to the Cloisters. The sculptor Roubilliac would come and admire his best work, and weep to think it was put too high to be appreciated.

Westwood Manor
Near Bradford-on-Avon, Wilts.

Westwood Manor is a delightful old manor house situated in its
own gardens in the sprawling village of Westwood, and standing on
high ground between the valleys of the Avon and Frome. This area of
Wiltshire was possibly the most favoured region for the quarrying of
good building stone, and so instead of using the flint, chalk cob, inferior brick, and the other makeshift materials of the downs, those
early builders used the local quarried stone to build this fascinating
but unpretentious manor house. Like many of its kind, it has suffered
the ravages of time, but its crumbling mortar and drunken doors add
a certain quality and charm.

The manor was built towards the end of the 15th century. Considerable alterations have been made since, which included the
embellishment of the interior with panelling and some excellent Jacobean plasterwork which may have been carried out in the 16th and
17th centuries. In the middle ages it belonged to Winchester Priory,
which leased it to tenants. At the dissolution of the monasteries it was
used to endow the Dean and Chapter of Winchester, and continued to
be leased to tenants until sold to a private owner by the Ecclesiastical
Commissioners in 1861.

The house was altered and decorated by a succession of tenants, of
whom the most celebrated were the Horton family, the prosperous
West of England woolmasters and clothiers, who occupied the manor
during the 16th century. It was the golden age of the West of England
broadcloth trade, families like the Longs, Methuens, Halls, Manvers,
and the Hortons formed an enterprising group of entrepreneurs, who
made large fortunes trading with the continent, reaching as far afield
as Florence. They built themselves fine stone houses which can be
seen today dotted around this western edge of Wiltshire, serving as
reminders of the opulent world of these industrious and cultivated
professional men. As if in expiation for their wealth these men built
those fine "cloth" churches with which Wiltshire is so well endowed.

The first member of the Horton family known to have lived at

Westwood Manor

Westwood was Thomas Horton. His father John Horton came from Lullington near Frome in Somerset, where he had carried on the trade as clothier. At the beginning of the 16th century he managed to obtain the lease of the Mill which was owned by the monks of Hinton Charterhouse on the River Frome just below Westwood, and so the Hortons came to Westwood.

Thomas inherited his father's clothingmaking business and became one of the richest clothiers in Wiltshire, owning property and land which stretched beyond Chippenham in the north, down to Trowbridge in the south. He married Mary, the daughter of Robert Lucas, a wealthy woolmaster from Steeple Ashton. The parish church of Bradford-on-Avon benefited considerably during his lifetime from his benevolence, and so it was fitting that Thomas should be buried there.

The Horton's alterations to the house can be seen in the dining room, which in the 16th century would have been the solar. The oriel is an attractive feature of this room, originally it consisted of six lights, but one was blocked up when later alterations were carried out in the 17th century. Alterations would have been carried out in the well proportioned bedroom situated above the dining-room, adding the panelling which is such an attractive feature of this room.

Toby Horton was the last of the Westwood Hortons, he had married Barbara the daughter of John Farewell, but Toby was heavily in debt about this time and was forced to dispose of his inheritance to his brother-in-law John Farewell, and so in 1616 the Farewells moved into Westwood, and further alterations were made. He remodelled much of the interior, and in doing so he made it more attractive and livable.

The Farewells left a daughter Elizabeth, who married a John Wallis. Their daughter, also called Elizabeth, married her cousin Henry Farewell. Elizabeth after the death of her husband continued to live at Westwood until 1722, when she died. She was the last of the Farewells, and Westwood unfortunately entered upon a period of decline.

The Listers seem to be the next owners who made any impact on Westwood. The manor remained in the ownership of the Dean and Chapter of Winchester until 1861 when it was transferred to the Ecclesiastical Commissioners, who eventually sold to a Mr. Tugwell of Crow Hall, Widcombe, Bath, who held the estates until 1911 when the house was sold to Mr. Edgar Graham Lister from Liverpool, and a member of the Diplomatic Corps.

In restoring Westwood Mr. Lister showed considerable understanding and skill, and much of what is seen today is owed to his meticulous taste. His other love was music, and among the many items which he bequeathed to the house are a spinet by Stephanus Keene of London, dating from the late 17th century, and an Italian virginal by Stephanus Mutinensis of Modena dated 1537. Mr. Lister gave the National Trust protective covenants over the Manor in 1943, and on his death in 1956, left the house and collection of furniture with an endowment, to the Trust.

Mention must be made here of the parish church of St. Mary which joins the Manor and forms a delightful group in this unspoilt corner of Wiltshire. The interior has much to commend it; the chancel is of the 13th century, and its windows show a fine display of late medieval painted glass. The nave was remodelled in the 18th century when it was provided with its attractive plaster ceiling. Attention is drawn to the stately tower with its domed turret and enriched parapet.

Widcombe Manor
Bath

Widcombe Manor known as the "Golden House" from the title of a book written by the author Horace Annesley Vachell when he was the owner. The novelist based his story on the honey-coloured mansion which originally belonged to the Lord of the Manor of Widcombe.

Early in the 18th century it passed to Philip Bennett, one time M.P. for Bath, who remodelled the house and refaced it in 1727 with Bath stone from Ralph Allen's stone quarries on Combe Down. Squire Bennett was a great friend of Henry Fielding, and his sister Sarah who lived next door at Widcombe Lodge. Fielding was a frequent

Widcombe Manor and Thomas à Becket Church

Thomas à Becket Church and Garden House

visitor to the Manor, and Bennett allowed him the use of one of the rooms to help him with his writing, and it is believed that Fielding's classic "Tom Jones" was written there.

Bennett's architect for the re-shaping of the Manor is uncertain, it could have been Thomas Greenway, but because of similarities of design with some early 18th century Bristol houses it is thought it is more likely to be the work of the Bristol architect John Strahan. There is doubt regarding the Manor's earlier architect. Walter Ison in his "Georgian Buildings of Bath" is being semantic when he writes, "Widcombe Manor House, both in design and execution, bears the impress of the cultivated mind of someone well acquainted with the earlier and somewhat French manner used by Vanbrugh in designing Castle Howard". Obviously from this description the architect would have to be a genius, and could well have been Inigo Jones filling the role, which has been suggested on more than one occasion. But Jones died in 1652, and only a handful of his buildings remain, and uncertainly hangs round some of the designs and drawings originally ascribed to him.

The courtyard leading into the Manor contains a handsome bronze fountain, believed to have come from the Renaissance Palazzo Grimani in Venice. The south front overlooking the courtyard is a gem, perfect in all respects, with emphasis on the pediment which contains an oval window flanked by garlands pouring from a cornucopiae. It displays an emotional style, and an exuberance usually associated with the Baroque. The interior is not lacking in artistic charm, and the fine panelled rooms, in particular the staircase, have responded significantly to careful remodelling by the new owners.

The Manorial buildings consist of a fine garden house, built later than the Manor, almost certainly not a Wood design, and hard by is the stable block and dove cote. After the death of Horace Vachell, his wife sold the Manor to Jeremy Fry, but kept this group of buildings which were tastefully converted to form a dwelling house quite separate from the Manor House, and which was renamed by Mrs. Vachell "Manor Farm".

In the cellars of the Manor the Rotork Engineering Company of Jeremy Fry commenced its embryonic life, to become one of Bath's foremost engineering enterprise. Jeremy Fry purchased the Manor in 1957 soon after the death of Horace Vachell. The Manor House has once again changed hands and is now owned by Mr. and Mrs. R. H. Warrender.

Standing before the Manorial gates one cannot fail to be impressed by the serene tranquillity of this village backwater of Bath. Directly across the street from the Manor stands the parish church of Thomas a Becket, built by William Birde, Prior of Bath Abbey, in 1502 on the site of an earlier Norman church, and further along Church Street is Widcombe Lodge, the home of Henry and Sarah Fielding for many years.

Wilton House
Near Salisbury, Wilts.

The year was 1521, the place, the waterfront at Bristol, a drunken young man of 25 years became innocently involved in a tavern brawl which resulted in him killing a man. He managed to escape and sailed for France where he enlisted in the army of Francois I. The young man was William Herbert who distinguished himself well whilst in the service of the King of France, and in 1534 he returned to England to serve Henry VIII. Henry was most impressed with Herbert and retained him as his personal bodyguard, and in this capacity Herbert came in contact with many of the ladies in waiting, and eventually married one, Anne Parr the daughter of Sir Thomas Parr a north country landowner.

Three queens later Henry married the shrewed but gentle Catherine Parr, the sister of Anne, and Herbert as the King's new brother-in-law had to be rewarded, and so a knighthood was given along with the monastic lands of the dissolved Abbey of Wilton.

William served his king diligently, sidetracking the treacherous game of politics, and using his nous to advantage, that by the end of Henry's reign he was well entrenched at Wilton, and like many of his ilk he had taken a full share of the monastic spoil. Wilton House was begun in the reign of Henry VIII and finished in the reign of Edward VI from designs claimed to be by Holbein.

On the death of Henry, Herbert found considerable favour with Edward VI, he entertained the young king at Wilton, and was granted for his trouble more land and the Earldom of Pembroke. Furthermore he switched his loyalty to the Duke of Northumberland, but this was a mistake, for England was faced with anarchy, and political ruin threatened Northumberland. The young king lay dying of consumption, and plans were being hatched to put Lady Jane Grey on the throne, in fact Pembroke joined with Northumberland in offering the crown to the Lady Jane, and marrying his son to her sister. It did not take him long to latch on to the disaster lying ahead; the tide was turning against Northumberland, and so he proclaimed for Mary,

Wilton House

annulled his son's marriage, and won his way into the new Queen's confidence. Northumberland lost his head. Within a very short time Pembroke was entertaining the envoys for Philip of Spain at Wilton, and even escorted Philip II of Spain to Winchester cathedral for his state marriage with Mary, which was conducted in the rites of the old church. In 1555 the notorious Marian persecution began, the accounts of which, in Fox's Book of Martyrs, were to make the blood of protestants run cold for many generations. The pendulum had now swung hard over in Pembroke's favour, but he was aging now, and Mary had only a short time to live. He changed course for the last time, and when Elizabeth came to the throne it is recorded that he carried her sword on her progress to London, and that she would dine with him often at his London mansion. Towards the end of his life he spent more time at Wilton where he concentrated on improving his house and estates.

Little remains of the Tudor building William knew, a porch detached from the house and known as the Holbein Porch survives, thanks to Inigo Jones who referred to the porch "as good architecture as any in England". Jones's Palladianism is much in evidence in the existing mansion. He began working for the third Earl of Pembroke when he was quite young, and in keeping with the fashion of the time, Jones accompanied the Earl on his Grand European Tour. The early background of Jones remains a mystery, in fact the exact date of his birth seems to be unrecorded, yet he received the patronage of the influential Herbert family, and to become the most powerful architectural mind England has ever produced.

103

Wilton House seems to present the story of Inigo Jones's career, you see here everything he lived for and struggled to achieve. It is a study of order, perfection and continuity, a house with a square plan and a quadrangle in the middle, and as a square it mirrored the all-round magnificence of the parkland. The creation of the gardens were largely the work of one man, Jones's former partner Isaac De Caus. He designed an elaborate Italianate garden with patterns and parterres to complement the architecture of his mentor, to give way in 1736 to the new cult of the landscape movement, where well manicured lawns and a stately sprawl of stone stretched down to the River Nadder, and where later Roger Morris added his delicate Palladian bridge.

Wilton House

Palladian Bridge, Wilton House

In 1647 fire destroyed a considerable part of the house which now needed reconstruction. The aging Inigo Jones was consulted, but in a fit of pique on being referred to as "Iniquity Jones" by Philip Herbert the fourth Earl he refused, but sent his nephew John Webb. However the plans for the restorations were Jones, his skills are seen in the faultless proportions of the Double Cube Room, which later became the inspiration behind the building of many of the state rooms of England's grand houses.

Around 1800 large scale structural alterations were made at Wilton by George Herbert, the eleventh Earl, who employed James Wyatt an architect of limited skills, to add his own style of Neo-Gothic to the Palladianism of Jones and Webb.

The marriage of Henry the second Earl to Mary Sidney, his third wife, brought not only considerable status by marrying into one of the main Elizabethan families – Cecil, Dudley, Walsingham, Howard, and the rest – but Mary was a woman of great learning, and at Wilton she took on the role of poet and patron, and encouraged men like Edmund Spenser, Ben Jonson, and Samuel Daniel to visit Wilton, and if tradition can be believed, Shakespeare and his company of players gave the first performance of "Twelfth Night", and "As you like it" here. Even Mary's physician, a Doctor Muffet, was assisted, but he was addicted to writing doggerel, and had an unsavoury reputation for prescribing spiders for all manner of ailments. However his daughter's phobia of spiders inspired him to write the famous nursery rhyme.

On the death of Henry, his eldest son William became the third

Earl, and with his brother Philip who later became the fourth Earl, they were well received at the Court of James I. The King was much addicted to favourites, especially handsome, quick-witted young men, and he regularly came to Wilton. William received honour upon honour, Knight of the Garter, Lord Chamberlain, and many others. Philip was made Earl of Montgomery, and when he married, the ceremony was held at Whitehall. Later he formed a deep and honourable friendship with Charles, the Prince of Wales, and it was on Charles's suggestion that Philip employed Van Dyck to paint the family portraits, which meant that the Herberts ended up with more Van Dyks than anyone else.

When Charles came to the throne, Philip was made Lord Chamberlain, but with the crises between Parliament and the Crown deepening, Philip hovered on the brink, undecided on which side to fall, however his mind was made up for him in the figure of William Laud, one time Bishop of Bath and Wells, who sided with the King. Philip had good reason to dislike this ecclesiastic, for it was Laud who beat him in the election for the Chancellorship of Oxford, and when he became primate and confidant of Charles, Philip finally made his decision and abandoned the King, and Wilton became a parliamentary bastion. It saw little action, a skirmish here and there. Fairfax and other parliamentary leaders stayed from time to time, otherwise the Civil War seemed to have by-passed Wilton.

In 1647 Philip was one of the Commissioners who received Charles from the Scots at Newcastle, and escorted him to Holmby House in Northamptonshire, but he had his atavistic sense to sheer clear of any involvement in the move to execute Charles, and so at the Restoration the Herberts kept their estates, whereas the regicides were not only losing theirs, but their heads as well.

Philip died in 1649, and was succeded by the fifth and sixth Earls, and for the first time Wilton entered into a period of mediocrity, but not for long, the seventh Earl, another Philip, brought back much of the colourful existence of the earlier years. He was a good-for-nothing wastrel, indulging in gambling and duelling, twice he was accused of murder and committed to the Tower. In 1675 he married Charles II's mistress's sister Henriette de Queronaille, and they had one daughter Charlotte who married the only son of the notorious Judge Jeffreys. Philip died in 1683, and the bulk of the family's art treasures were sold to pay his debts, while Thomas, his brother, inherited the title and became the eighth Earl.

It was the age which saw the continued flowering of artistic genius, the age of patronage, where the arts were encouraged as never before. Thomas entered into the full spirit of this period. Inspired with restoring Wilton's treasures, he travelled widely, and collected wisely, and had the satisfaction of possessing a picture painted by each artist of all the Italian schools. To encourage the weaving of carpets he introduced French weavers to Wilton, who were supposed to be Louis XV's skilled personal weavers.

Wilton House

Thomas was among the peers who offered the Crown to William, a successful ploy which paid off later, because he was made Lord High Admiral, a member of the Privy Council, and later still he was made Lord Lieutenant of Ireland and a Knight of the Garter. He married three times and on each occasion the fortunes of the Herbert family prospered. Thomas died in 1733 and Henry the eldest son of his first marriage became the ninth Earl.

Henry the "architect Earl" friend of Lord Burlington and William Kent, started life as a soldier, but like Burlington he preferred the arts, and so leaving the service of the king, he became an architect. Assisted by his clerk of works Roger Morris he built the beautiful Palladian bridge across the River Nadder. Horace Walpole considered his architectural taste faultless, better even than Burlington or Kent.

Another Henry, the tenth Earl, followed his father in 1749 and entered the army and became a general, and a leading authority on military equitation. He married in 1756 the daughter of the Duke of Marlborough, but because of his raffish character, and his association with a certain Kitty Hunter, the marriage was far from satisfactory. He had one son George who became the eleventh Earl on the death of Henry in 1794.

George was so obsessively finicky that he listed every small item of expenditure, and he could even remember the wages paid to each of his servants, not a very difficult exercise in those days considering the pittance each was paid. In 1808 he married his second wife Catherine, daughter of the Count Simon Woronzow, the Russian Ambassador in London.

It was left to Reginald the fifteenth Earl to alter the worst of Wyatt's gothic which included the library and dining-room. He entertained Queen Elizabeth II here in 1953, and became a great friend of Churchill who as Prime Minister during the Second World War made regular vists to Wilton for the house at that time was Southern Command H.Q.'s.

Henry the present and seventeenth Earl of Pembroke, the fourteenth Earl Of Montgomery was born in 1939 and married Miss Claire Pelly, daughter of Mr. Douglas Pelly, a former High Sheriff of Essex. Wilton House has its place in the history of England, it is a story of one family's devotion and care. It remains today one of the great English houses still existing in private hands.

Worspring or Woodspring Priory
Weston-super-Mare, Avon

It was a cold December evening in the year 1170, the scene, the precincts of Canterbury Cathedral, dusk had already fallen, and in the distance could be heard the monks chanting their evensong. The stillness of the night was suddenly shattered as the door leading to the cloisters was rudely pushed open admitting four knights and their retainers, demanding to see Thomas Becket. The tall and dominating figure of the Archbishop appeared, he had no intention of evading these men, and he demanded to know their business. He was accused by the knights of treachery to the king and the realm, and with the words "You shall die" ringing throughout the cathedral, the four advanced towards the priest, swords flashed in the fading light, and in seconds the mutilated body of this "turbulent priest" – the words of Henry II – lay dead on the blood-spattered cathedral stones. England and Europe were outraged by his murder and within three years the Pope gave his consent to Becket's canonisation. England's greatest vandal, Henry VIII, when he broke with Rome visited Canterbury Cathedral and ordered the destruction of Becket's shrine and tomb.

However in a remote corner of Avon County, a solitary place even today, there stands a reminder of Becket's martyrdom, the remains of Woodspring Priory. Bungalow development threatens to intrude on the privacy of this one time religious establishment, but fortunately a few years back the National Trust with the help of the Landmark Trust was able to purchase the estate, now known as Woodspring, which also includes Middle Hope, a two-mile stretch of coastline, and the headland of Sandpoint. The West Country has the dubious honour of claiming all four of Becket's murderers. Reginald FitzUrse was born in the parish of Williton near Minehead, and Richard Le Brett held the manor of Sampford Brett a mile away. Both Hugh de Morville and William de Tracy came from Devon, where people would recite the rhyme "The Tracys, the Tracys, the Wind in their faces", which referred to Tracy's attempt to sail to the Holy Land to expiate his

Woodspring Priory

crime, and the fishermen would hear his voice wailing in the night winds.

Forty years after Becket's death Woodspring Priory was founded by William de Courtenay, who according to some historians was the grandson of William de Tracy, while some prefer to think that the evidence points more directly to FitzUrse as the grandsire. However the daughter and grand-daughter of Le Brett bequeathed lands to the Priory, and in 1210 its founder announced to the Bishop of Bath and Wells its dedication to the Virgin and St. Thomas of Canterbury. It was a very small community at Woodspring, eight Victorine Canons and a handful of monks belonging to the order of St. Augustine, probably attached to the Abbey of St. Augustine in Bristol. During its 300 years of existence the Priory extended its ownership of land, by gifts from the relatives of the murderers, down to Worle, Locking and out as far as Winscombe and Puxton.

There is of course the legend of the Becket Cup, now in Taunton Museum. In 1536 had come a move which affected the people everywhere. Cromwell and his agents on behalf of their royal master Henry VIII had begun the plunder and suppression of the monasteries. The shrines of the saints were desecrated, their ashes and relics cast out. The broad acres of the abbeys were given over to a new class of grasping landowners, who enclosed the common lands and hardened their hearts against the poor.

In 1534 the Prior of Woodspring had submitted to the will of Henry, but its value at that time was a derisory £87, and so their submission did not save their dissolution in 1536. Foreseeing the fate of their Priory the monks carried their most precious possession − a wooden cup holding the blood of Thomas Becket − to the parish church of Kewstoke where it was found in 1849 during alterations to the church behind a sculptured figure which had been fixed to the north wall by the Prior Roger Tormynton. The cup was stained with a man's blood.

The Priory had now been restored, and presents an attractive group of 14th century buildings after long use as part of a farmer's home. It still stands sentinel, as it has done for over 700 years, sheltering in a turfy hollow surrounded by marshy meadows on one side, and by sea and sand dunes on the other.

Index